How to
Deal With Parents
Who Are
Angry,
Troubled,
Afraid, or
JUST PLAIN CRAZY

Elaine K. McEwan

How to Deal With Parents Who Are

Angry,
Troubled,
Afraid, or
JUST PLAIN CRAZY

Second Edition

CORWIN PRESS
A Sage Publications Company
Thousand Oaks, California

For information:

Corwin Press
A Sage Publications Company
2455 Teller Road
Thousand Oaks, California 91320
www.corwinpress.com

SAGE Publications Ltd
1 Oliver's Yard
55 City Road
London EC1Y 1SP
United Kingdom

Sage Publications India Pvt. Ltd.
B-42, Panchsheel Enclave
Post Box 4109
New Delhi 110 017 India

Printed in the United States of America

Library of Congress Cataloging-in-Publication Data

McEwan, Elaine K., 1941-
How to deal with parents who are angry, troubled, afraid, or just plain crazy / Elaine K. McEwan.—2nd ed.
    p. cm.
Includes bibliographical references and index.
ISBN 1-4129-0443-9 (hardcover) — ISBN 1-4129-0444-7 (pbk.)
    1. Home and school—United States. 2. Education—Parent participation—United States. 3. Parents—United States—Psychology. I. Title.
LC225.3.M395 2005
371.1′03—dc22

                    2004012311

This book is also available in audio through the Recording for the Blind & Dyslexic. For more information on how to obtain a copy, contact (866) 732-3585 or www.RFBD.org.

This book is printed on acid-free paper.

05   06   07   08   09   10   9   8   7   6   5   4   3   2   1

Acquisitions Editor:	Robert D. Clouse
Editorial Assistant:	Jingle Vea
Production Editor:	Kristen Gibson
Copy Editor:	Marilyn Power Scott
Proofreader:	Kevin Gleason
Typesetter:	C&M Digitals (P) Ltd.
Cover Designer:	Michael Dubowe

Contents

Preface

In the fall of 1983, I was hired for my first principalship at an elementary school in a far western suburb of Chicago. Armed with a newly acquired doctoral degree in administration and "dressed for success," I eagerly anticipated helping teachers improve their instructional effectiveness, setting high expectations for students, and developing curriculum. Somewhere along the way, I must have missed the course to prepare me for the almost daily encounters I would have with parents who were angry, troubled, afraid, or in some cases, "just plain crazy." Although the latter group was certainly a small minority, there were enough parents in my school (and I'm sure yours is no different) who seemed to leave all reason and common sense at the front door as they stormed the office. Dealing with these moms and dads often made me feel like I was picking my way through a minefield, ignorant of where the next explosion would occur.

Oh, I'd had the requisite school-community relations course. But the syllabus contained nothing about marriage and family counseling or conflict resolution. I started to think that perhaps I'd earned the wrong degree, but it was too late. The problems were on my doorstep from day one. I remember one incident in Technicolor. It was Halloween, and the excitement in the hallways was palpable. A parade headlined the afternoon's festivities, and I had my costume hung on the back of the office door. I would change during the lunch hour.

My secretary pronounced my Busy Bee getup perfect. "Great choice. You're always buzzing around," she said. I was too distracted to reflect on exactly what she meant and headed to the hallway as the children came in from lunch recess. I was greeted with compliments and calls of delight. My black leotards and turtleneck were topped with an oversized garbage bag of the same color, striped with wide yellow tape. Tightly secured at my arms, legs, and neck, the bag made a perfect bee body. The piece de resistance of my costume was a headpiece on which golden spheres bobbed from springy wires.

After two months on the job, I was feeling confident, and I looked forward to greeting the many parents who traditionally attended the parade. My euphoria lasted all of fifteen seconds before I was blindsided by a mom I'd already come to know and love. She sailed into the office with eyes blazing. Fortunately, she was armed with nothing but her tongue, but she proceeded to deliver a lashing that could have bested any belt or razor strop. "No one is going to treat my child like that," she screamed. "Do something." I longed for a genie to appear and calm this crazed woman, but no one came to my rescue. I took her into my office and elicited the story. She had just happened to be walking down the hall when her third-grade daughter's class went by on its way to the rest rooms. Naturally, the classroom teacher selected this precise moment to give the aforementioned daughter a good dressing down for all the world to see and hear, including mom— an unfortunate juxtaposition of circumstances, to be sure. I wished at that moment for an alien spaceship to land on the playground and transport teacher, child, and parent to outer space. They were all out of control. What was I to do? Desperate for any solution, I suggested a meeting after school with the teacher. Mom insisted that her husband, who was only a phone call away, come immediately to school and talk with me. Apparently, she felt that he could put me in my place. He arrived shortly, gave me the once-over in my bee costume, and slumped into a corner in my office, saying nothing. Obviously, he'd learned that it was best to be seen and not heard. Dressed in camouflage that did not appear to be part of a Halloween costume, he looked like he might just pull a gun from beneath his jacket at any moment.

Once again, mom recounted the story of her daughter's humiliation in vivid detail. The retelling only fueled her anger, and she demanded that I fire the teacher on the spot. Save for tenure, it was a tempting thought. Still no word from dad. We agreed that we would meet with the teacher after school to gather more information; dad nodded his assent. He eyeballed me head to toe one last time and quietly followed his wife from the office.

As soon as the parade ended, I made a quick change out of my costume, raced to the third-grade hallway, and briefed the teacher on my tentative plan for the meeting. "Stay calm, listen, and then be prepared to apologize for losing your cool in front of the world," I advised. "Above all, don't be defensive or raise your voice." I was grateful it was Friday, and I'd have the weekend to recover.

The meeting went as well as could be expected. We all agreed that the daughter's behavior was unacceptable. We all agreed (even the teacher) that the teacher's behavior was unacceptable. I even coaxed a small apology out of mom for being so disruptive and inappropriate earlier. Still no word from dad. He seemed content to watch from the sidelines. It was nearly 5:00 p.m. when everyone filed out of my office. Dad brought up the rear. Just before we reached the door, he leaned over, and with a wink, whispered in my ear, "I liked you better in your bee costume." A sexist remark to be sure, but for me, it was the perfect ending to a "no good, very bad, horrible day" in the life of an average principal.

In the years that followed, my meetings with parents who were angry, troubled, afraid, or totally out of control would become commonplace. I no longer developed sweaty palms, a racing heart, and blotchy skin. I became a confident and capable administrator who had acquired the skills to calm the angriest and to counsel the most troubled. In the pages ahead, I'll share the strategies that have helped me deal with challenging parents. You will learn how to handle "close encounters of the parental kind" with confidence, and although I can't promise a money-back guarantee, I'm quite sure you'll gradually feel the satisfaction that comes from finding solutions to difficult problems.

MY DEFINITION OF "CRAZY"

When I first suggested the title of this book as a possibility in 1997, the rare objections to it came from individuals who worked in the mental health field and had never been school principals. They were concerned, and rightly so, with the stigma attached to the term *crazy* when applied to individuals with mental illness. Educators, however, resonated with the term. They had all been verbally or even physically assaulted by parents who were totally out of control. In this second edition, as in the first, I use the term tongue in cheek, to specifically refer to *irrational behavior that is upsetting to others—whatever its cause.* Parents can of course be angry, troubled, and afraid *without* being irrational. In fact, there are dozens of situations that demand a strong dose of righteous indignation. It is when parental behavior crosses the line from being assertive and appropriate to being dangerous, hostile, demeaning, threatening, manipulative, or aggressive (either in upfront *or* passive ways) that it not only becomes "crazy" but also tends to make educators somewhat "crazy" themselves. I wish to be sensitive to my colleagues, friends, and family members who are dealing with depression and anxiety and any other disorders of which I am not aware, and I intend no offense or prejudice.

WHO THIS BOOK IS FOR

I have written *How to Deal With Parents Who Are Angry, Troubled, Afraid, and Just Plain Crazy* for the following audiences:

- Principals at every level who want to enhance their personal effectiveness in working with parents to build productive learning communities
- Supervisors, mentors, or coaches whose goal is to encourage the principals with whom they work to become more confident and successful in their relationships with parents
- College and university teachers of courses in school-community relations or the principalship who wish to introduce prospective principals to the challenges of interacting positively with a diverse parent community
- Central office administrators who are expected to deal with a wide variety of angry parents in their job roles as

well as supervise, coach, and mentor principals in their districts

- Classroom teachers who are considering the principalship and wish to broaden their perspective regarding their interactions and relationships with parents

SPECIAL FEATURES OF THE BOOK

The second edition of *How to Deal With Parents Who Are Angry, Troubled, Afraid, and Just Plain Crazy* contains the following special features and additions:

- An enhanced section of strategies for dealing with the ever-increasing population of parents who fall into the irrational and out-of-control category
- Updated references and examples
- A brand-new conclusion containing Ten Goals-at-a-Glance to keep your school-community relations on target
- An updated and easy-to-administer Healthy School Checklist to help you determine if your school's culture and climate encourage parents or push them over the edge
- A comprehensive facilitator's guide printed on shaded paper that includes energizers, think-alouds, suggestions for role-playing, and questions for dialogue

OVERVIEW OF THE CONTENTS

Chapter 1 describes the parents of today's children and discusses the critical issues that cause misunderstandings in schools. Chapter 2 includes a variety of responsive strategies for defusing parents who are angry, troubled, afraid, and irrationally out of control. This chapter will help you to ease the fears, calm the troubled spirits, and shut down the angry outbursts of parents so that you can move to exploration and action in the next chapter.

Chapter 3 explains numerous helpful exploration and action strategies, including a seven-step problem-solving process to help ensure the quick solution of the problems that worry and trouble parents. Chapter 4 is titled Creating and Nurturing a Healthy School. After reading this chapter, you will be able to analyze your school environment to discover whether you and your faculty are on your way to health and happiness or are unwittingly creating a dysfunctional "school family." Chapter 5 includes dozens of proactive things you can do to develop a supportive and involved parent community. The conclusion summarizes the key points of the book and is designed to help you keep your mission focused on accentuating the positive in your relationships with parents. The facilitator's guide at the back of the book is designed to help you facilitate a book study group, provide lesson plans for the next university class you teach, or suggest ideas for personal reflection and goal setting. Throughout the book you will find quotations from teachers and parents who, while willing to have their experiences and opinions included in the book, wished to remain anonymous.

ACKNOWLEDGMENTS

A special thank you to the educators across the country who have shared with me the ways in which they have used the first edition of this book to improve the effectiveness of their interactions with angry parents. If not for their enthusiasm and support, this second edition would not have been written. One of the delights of being an author in this age of cyber-communication is receiving e-mails from readers. If you would like to ask a question, share a story or experience based on your implementation of an idea in this book, *or* point out an error, please contact me at emcewan@ elainemcewan.com, and I will answer you as quickly as I can. Or visit my Web site: http://www.elainemcewan.com.

This book is dedicated to Gracia Alkema, publisher emeritus of Corwin Press. The first edition was one of the earliest books I wrote for Corwin, and she stood behind me and the concept 100 percent. I am grateful for her editorial judgment and publishing savvy as well as our eight-year friendship.

As always, I owe a special debt of gratitude to my husband and business partner, E. Raymond Adkins. Those readers who have attended my workshops and presentations know what a steady and supportive presence he is. His wisdom and common sense are the final arbiters of what goes into all of my books.

In addition, Corwin Press gratefully acknowledges the contributions of the following people:

Rosemary L. Young
Principal
Watson Lane Elementary
    School
NAESP President-Elect
Louisville, KY

Gloria Kumagai
Principal
Museum Magnet
    Elementary School
Golden Valley, MN

Gina Segobiano
Principal/Superintendent
Signal Hill School District
Belleville, IL

Candace Stevens
Principal
Jacob Wismer
    Elementary School
Portland, OR

Diane Mierzwik
Author, Teacher
Parkview Middle School
Yucaipa, CA

Marilyn J. Montgomery
Author, Professor
Florida International
    University
Miami, FL

Charles M. Jaksec, III
Author, School Social Worker
Hillsborough County School
    District
Tampa, FL

Jean Cheng Gorman
Author
San Francisco, CA

Gwen L. Rudney
Author, Associate
    Professor of Education
Coordinator of
    Elementary Education
University of Minnesota
Morris, MN

About the Author

 **Elaine K. McEwan** is a partner and educational consultant with The McEwan-Adkins Group, offering workshops in instructional leadership, team building, and raising reading achievement, K–12. A former teacher, librarian, principal, and assistant superintendent for instruction in a suburban Chicago school district, she is the author of more than thirty-five books for parents and educators. Her Corwin Press titles include *Leading Your Team to Excellence: Making Quality Decisions* (1997), *7 Steps to Effective Instructional Leadership* (1998), *The Principal's Guide to Attention Deficit Hyperactivity Disorder* (1998), *How to Deal with Parents Who Are Angry, Troubled, Afraid, or Just Plain Crazy* (1998), *The Principal's Guide to Raising Reading Achievement* (1998), *Counseling Tips for Elementary School Principals* (1999) with Jeffrey A. Kottler, *Managing Unmanageable Students: Practical Solutions for Educators* (2000) with Mary Damer, *The Principal's Guide to Raising Math Achievement* (2000), *Raising Reading Achievement in Middle and High Schools: Five Simple-to-Follow Strategies for Principals* (2001), *Ten Traits of Highly Effective Teachers: How to Hire, Mentor, and Coach Successful Teachers* (2001), *Teach Them ALL to Read: Catching the Kids Who Fall through the Cracks* (2002), *7 Steps to Effective Instructional Leadership, Second Edition* (2003), *Making Sense of Research: What's Good, What's Not, and How to Tell the Difference* (2003) with Patrick J. McEwan, *Ten Traits of Highly Effective Principals: From Good to Great Performance* (2003), and *Seven Strategies of Highly Effective Readers: Using Cognitive Research to Boost K–8 Achievement* (2004).

McEwan was honored by the Illinois Principals Association as an outstanding instructional leader, by the Illinois State Board of Education with an Award of Excellence in the Those Who Excel Program, and by the National Association of Elementary School Principals as the National Distinguished Principal from Illinois for 1991. She received her undergraduate degree in education from Wheaton College and advanced degrees in library science (MA) and educational administration (EdD) from Northern Illinois University. She lives with her husband and business partner E. Raymond Adkins in Oro Valley, Arizona. Visit her Web site at www.elainemcewan.com where you can learn more about her writing and workshops and enroll in online seminars based on her books, or contact her directly at emcewan@elainemcewan.com.

Why So Many Parents Are Angry, Troubled, Afraid, or Just Plain Crazy

Seek first to understand, before you seek to be understood.

—Stephen Covey (1989, p. 235)

There's a lot of questioning, blaming, and downright hostility out there. And it's going both ways. Parents aren't as willing as they used to be to support the schools, either philosophically or financially, and educators in the trenches are becoming more vocal about parents' shortcomings. A Public Agenda (2003) poll reports that an overwhelming majority of teachers (81%) believe that parents are at fault for not making their children study hard and behave well, but on the other hand, some educators are beginning to label parents as "helicopters" (Advising Forum, 2003; Definition of helicopter parent, 2004) and "enablers" for their hovering inter-ference and indulgent overinvolvement both in and out of school (American Society of Professional Education, 2004). Nearly half of the superintendents polled say they personally spend too much time dealing with complaining parents. And the relationship between parents and school principals is not particularly rosy, either. *The MetLife Survey of the American Teacher: An Examination of School Leadership* (MetLife, 2003), reports that "half of the parents polled do not feel that the principal-parent relationship at their child's school is supportive, mutually respectful or friendly" (p. 46). Although the principals who were surveyed reported that they frequently meet with parents, this is not the parents' perception (p. 49). "Parents do not feel that they are among the principal's priorities, but principals do not seem to be aware of parents' dissatisfaction" (p. 61). At a time when parental support is essential for raising achievement standards, far too many parents feel estranged and unwelcome at school.

I've personally experienced school problems from both sides of the desk. I've been angry, troubled, and afraid. I can also think of at least one occasion when my daughter's principal probably muttered, "That woman is crazy," under her breath as I left the office steaming over an unresolved problem. I know how parents feel when they have a problem and find that no one is willing to address it. As an administrator, I've also encountered my share of parents whose overwrought emotions and aggressive behavior stood in the way of seeing issues clearly and addressing problems squarely. Educators cannot afford to ignore distraught parents, for when moms and dads are unhappy with the schools (and the people who run them), their kids pay the price. One of our key responsibilities as instructional leaders is to maintain positive attitudes toward students, staff, and parents to ensure that all children can learn. This includes "demonstrating concern and openness in the consideration of student, teacher, and/or parent problems and participating in the resolution of such problems where appropriate" and "modeling appropriate human relations skills" (McEwan, 2003a, p. 180). We are the frontline interpreters of educational policy. We are responsible for the quality and effectiveness of classroom teachers. We are "accountable for fostering the kind of school climate where the dignity and worth of all individuals without regard to appearance, race, creed, sex, ability or disability, or social status is of paramount importance" (McEwan, 2003a, p. 172).

Although dozens of distressed and disturbed parents may walk into your office, few should leave feeling the same way. Will they always get what they want? No. Will you always agree with them? Of course not. But should you listen carefully to everything they have to say and engage in meaningful problem solving with them? Always. It's easy to be gracious and warm to parents who are positive and cooperative, but how do you handle those who question and accuse? First of all, try to understand why they feel the way they do. In many cases, their distress is well founded. I must warn you that you may be tempted to close this book in frustration before you finish this chapter. The litany of scenarios that disturb parents can make for depressing reading. But even when you're not responsible for parents' hostile feelings, you have to deal with them, and how better to do that than armed with information and understanding?

THE PARENTS OF TODAY

Gone are the "good old days" when educators were revered and respected for their wisdom and position by parents. Now, we have to earn our respect the old-fashioned way: Work for it. As one beleaguered administrator told me, "Twenty years ago, all I had to do was keep the teachers and the parents happy. Now, I need to get results" (McEwan, 2003b, p. xiv). And today's parents *are* a different breed—less trusting of our educational platitudes and quick to point out what they perceive to be stupidity, inconsistency, stonewalling, or incompetence in both administrators and teachers. Parents don't want us to select curricula, hire teachers, and make policies that impact their children without using common sense, sound reasons, and scientific research to inform our decisions. They resent being told to "just trust us." Here's a small sample of the kinds of parents you may find waiting in your office on any given day.

Less Respectful of Authority

Lack of respect by parents shows up everywhere—in their exchanges with teachers, in public meetings, and especially in how they treat administrators. Angry exchanges at school board meetings are commonplace, and courtesies that once were taken for granted are now unusual and noteworthy. Of course, educators aren't the only middle managers dealing with a frustrated and hostile clientele. But when one's children are at risk, emotions overheat and tempers flare more readily than they do over car repairs or changing a cell phone plan. Dealing with parents who lack respect for us means that before we can move to problem solving, we must first establish rapport and gain respect.

More Educated About Education

When the first edition of this book was published in 1997, I investigated a number of books geared to an audience of affluent parents, eager to find the inside track to ensuring preferential treatment and the best teachers for their children in public schools (Harrington & Young, 1993; Keogh, 1996; Nemko & Nemko, 1986). A second generation of books, written by and for African American parents, now echoes the themes from the earlier volumes—be proactive, hold high expectations, and become involved in all matters of schooling (Brown, 2003). And another category of books by African American authors seeks to illuminate the cultural issues of language and class as they relate to minority student achievement (Hale, 2001; Kunjufu, 2002).

In addition, parents of today, empowered by Google and informed by the public debates surrounding the No Child Left Behind Act (2002) are informed about drop-out rates, disaggregated data, standardized testing, and comparative school and district ratings. Hassel and Hassel (2004) use the term "picky parents" to refer to a group of well educated and discriminating parents who are informed and knowledgeable about school options and what to look for in a school. Experienced administrators have their own definition of a picky parent—someone who is never quite happy.

Angrier Than Ever

Far too many parents subscribe to the notion that the healthiest way to handle their enmity against educators is to "get it off their chests" and "tell it like they see it." Unfortunately, for educators who are the recipients of these angry tirades, the supposed cathartic effects of getting mad are only a myth. Angry parents don't turn into positive people once they've unloaded on the principal. In fact, as you no doubt know from your own experiences, parents end up with more anger, not less, when they continually unload their vitriol on others (Berkowitz, 1970; Lewis & Bucher, 1992; Warren & Kurlychek, 1981).

Cynical and Distrustful

Today's parents are a reflection of our society at large, unwilling to trust institutions that have taken their trust and misused it. They don't believe it just because we say so. They want to see budgets, curricula, test scores, and research. They question our judgment, quibble with our reasons, and demand more information than they ever wanted in the past. They have read books with titles like *The Feel-Good Curriculum: The Dumbing Down of America's Kids in the Name of Self-Esteem* (Stout, 2001) and *The Conspiracy of Ignorance: The Failure of the American Public Schools* (Gross, 2000), and some even believe that school administrators are part of some vast conspiracy to take over the minds of their children.

Activists

As an administrator in today's schools, be ready for parent involvement that is far more sophisticated than making cupcakes for the bake sale (Bradley, 1997). The Internet provides an ideal venue for parents who question what is going on in their local schools and want to check it out with others. If you have never visited an education consumers' Web site, head to the Illinois Loop (2004) that "helps to provide information on issues in Illinois education to the parents who are consumers of that education, to the taxpayers who pay for it, and to everyone who wants to restore quality to Illinois schools." And a national consumers' network provides a forum for parents who have questions about curriculum, pedagogy, and policies (Education Consumers Network, 2004).

In his book, *Is There a Public for the Public Schools?* David Matthews (1996) writes that the public has become deeply ambivalent about the role of public schools. People want to support them but also want their children to receive a good education, and increasingly, they see the two goals as conflicting. Many parents respond to this feeling by pulling their children out of the public schools after experiencing frustration at being stonewalled over issues they deem nonnegotiable, but surprisingly, these same parents often remain deeply involved in community activism, even running and winning seats on the school board or forming school watch-dog groups (Informed Residents of Reading, 2004).

Stressed

Many of today's parents lead complicated lives replete with daily planners, cell phones, and nannies. Or they fall into another category of working parents, those who are juggling three part-time jobs to stay alive. Well-off or struggling, huge numbers of parents rarely have enough time to do the things they should be doing, and finding fifteen minutes of quality time per day per child is a futile dream. These parents are counting on the schools to take up the slack. The time bind that most families face translates into increased school stress for students, teachers, and administrators. Parents want educators to handle all of their children's problems at school without bothering them at work; latchkey kids and blended families add further stress to the system.

Worried and Fearful

Parents who see education as the answer to a better future for their children are concerned that watered-down curricula, lack of standards, poorly trained or incompetent teachers, and out-of-control student behavior will deprive their children of the skills they need to succeed in life. They see the schools in their neighborhoods failing to provide discipline, basic skills, and moral values and are worried that even if they exercise the No Child Left Behind Act (2002) option to choose another school, it's all too little and too late.

WHAT'S BEHIND THE EPIDEMIC?

There are four big reasons for the epidemic of angry, troubled, afraid, or just outrageous parents:

- The world in which we live is filled with influences and circumstances that often foster hostility, rage, and out-of-control behavior.
- Educators unwittingly or even intentionally upset parents with the things they do and say.
- Education is characterized by broad swings of philosophy and methodology, a steady stream of innovations that often defy logic, and constant pleas to the public for more money to solve its problems, creating the belief among some that educators don't know what they're doing.
- Parents have pervasive family dynamics or personal psychological, emotional, and behavioral problems that impact the ways in which they interact with almost everyone, but most especially educators.

Reason 1: The World Is a Stressful Place

When I started teaching school several decades ago, life was simple. All of our students went home for lunch, and teachers enjoyed a quiet hour to talk with colleagues or plan lessons. I even had time during my lunch hour to wash and dry my clothes at a nearby laundromat. Teachers nowadays have scarcely thirty minutes in which to wolf down sandwiches while they supervise the cafeteria and fit in calls to upset parents from their cell phones. Most administrators don't "do lunch" at all.

Today's world is stressful, fast paced, and fragmented. C. Leslie Charles (1999) suggests ten reasons why "everybody is so cranky," and several of them help to explain why so many of our parents are angry, troubled, afraid, and out of control. Unfortunately, administrators and teachers are subject to the same societal and cultural forces, perhaps explaining why quiet conversations in which educators and parents listen to one another and come to mutually agreeable solutions are becoming more rare.

Here are just three of the trends described by Charles (1999) that definitely make us all a little crankier: compressed time, communication overload, and disconnectedness (pp. 10–11). Our days speed by like a fast-forwarding video; sleep deprived and hyped on sugar and caffeine, we're assaulted by nonstop communication. We're bombarded with voice mail from multiple phones, e-mail from multiple computers, and express mail from Airborne, Fed-Ex, UPS, and USPS, to say nothing of the calls from telemarketers that jam our phone lines and the spam and viruses that invade our computers. Unfortunately, this communication overload does little to build meaningful bonds between people since we hardly ever talk face to face.

Reason 2: Educators Do Things That Upset Parents

The list of ways that educators distress parents is a long one, and although you may not be guilty of doing any of the things listed here, you will undoubtedly encounter parents who, based on their past experiences with other educators, will treat you as though you have. Before you get defensive and start making excuses, try to understand these parents. Be aware of the following reasons why parents are blowing their proverbial tops more frequently:

Failure to Communicate

This is the number one reason why parents get mad. Consider the principal who, two weeks into the school year, was authorized to hire another third grade teacher to alleviate overcrowding. Jubilant at solving the problem, the principal never stopped to consider the necessity of notifying the parents and students who were being reshuffled and displaced. Kids were upset, parents were furious, and the principal is still licking the wounds.

Making major changes without giving parents input or even a heads-up has a way of making them seethe. Although public hearings, newsletters, advisory councils, and opinion polls do take a lot of time and don't always give people what they want, information sharing and discussion can defuse anger and quell rumors. In a small eastern community, one solution to overcrowding was to move the kindergarten class to a vacant high school classroom. Imagine the rumors of children being plowed down in the parking lot by power-crazed teens in hot rods. Consider the possibility of mere infants exposed to teens smoking and making out in the hallways. Or even worse, the prospect of drugs being offered to fresh-faced five-year-olds. After public meetings and joint problem solving, an early childhood education program staffed by high school students (who received credit) proved to be an innovative educational offering that everyone could support.

If a lack of communication on the administrative level annoys many parents, failure to keep information flowing from teachers to parents makes all moms and dads mad. They hate surprises. In response to a public outcry in one school district where parents were constantly blindsided by report cards with failing grades, the superintendent mandated midterm reports.

Educators constantly talk about the importance of communication, says parent activist Daniel Wolff (2002) in an *Education Week* essay: *"'We have to improve our communication skills'* is a favorite [edu-speak statement] among administrators. When it turns out there's no publicity for a meeting on how children get into advanced classes—or when the $5000 raise for the director of special education is passed in private—the district will say it has to improve its communication skills. A good rule of thumb for parents is to assume that when you hear this phrase, you've stumbled on a secret."

Circling the Wagons

Automatically backing teachers against parents and kids, without really hearing the issue described from the parents' perspective or talking to the children involved, ranks high on the list of things that make parents furious. I call this practice "circling the wagons." Many teachers believe that their administrator's first responsibility is to back them, no matter what they do. But when teachers are abusing children (psychologically or physically), wasting children's time, or freelancing with the curriculum, parents are hard pressed to understand why an administrator would defend or cover up for the wrongdoers.

Consider a case in Berkeley, California, where the school district paid $1.15 million to settle a lawsuit brought by nine female students and five of their mothers that claimed the district failed to investigate sexual abuse complaints against a teacher. Because the teacher in question was a popular one, no one believed the students, and the wagons continued to circle even as the students were testifying against him in court (Walsh, 1996).

Stonewalling and Spinelessness

Saying you'll do something about a problem and then doing nothing or promising to call a parent back and then misplacing the message are other practices that make parents climb the walls. Knowing that a disciplinary problem exists (e.g., bullying on the playground, smoking in the washrooms, rebellion in the lunchroom) or that a personnel issue is approaching an emergency (e.g., a teacher is harassing a student, instruction is ineffective, a classroom is out of control) and choosing to ignore it out of fear, indifference, or just plain indecision is a risky business.

In a decision by a nine-member federal jury, a school district in Ashland, Wisconsin, was found guilty of discrimination against a gay high school student by failing to protect him from the verbal and physical brutality of his classmates. The case was settled out of court for nearly $1 million. This incident is a disturbing example of what can happen when pretending nothing is wrong becomes a way of life for administrators. Although the boy's parents repeatedly brought their complaints to school district officials, the abuse their son suffered at the hands of his classmates continued over a six-year period ("A Lesson," 1996; "Gay Student Wins," 1996).

Assumptions and Stereotypes

Having labels put on us because of marital status, religious beliefs, sex, color, ethnicity, or socioeconomic status makes us all angry, parents included, and justifiably so. Just because I go to church and want my children to learn phonics, don't label me as a right-wing conservative. If I'm a single parent, don't assume that I neglect my children, and just because I'm poor, don't type me as a lazy good-for-nothing.

Defensiveness

Getting defensive whenever a parent questions our actions or motives is a natural, *but unwise*, reaction. Our behavior will surely escalate what could have been a calm discussion into an angry exchange on both sides. When we get defensive, we appear guilty, stupid, and dishonest. All of these postures only serve to inflame a parent who only wanted answers or explanations.

Breaking Promises

In the heat of the moment, principals sometimes make promises they can't keep. *"The bus will stop right at your front door."* Parents later find out that the bus stop is a half a mile away. *"Oh, yes, we'll be hiring a middle-school band director for next year."* Parents read in the newspaper that the school board decided to double up music teachers at its last meeting. *"Even if we don't have a full class of students, we'll still have that fast-paced math class."* As it turns out, there's only one student, and the class is canceled. Whether or not you are the individual to blame for the change in plans (and you usually aren't), the angry parent will forever remember *your* broken promise and blame *you.*

Intimidation, Control, Power, and Blame

There are dozens of ways that we educators can subtly intimidate parents; most are unintentional but nonetheless damaging. We send parents notices of meetings without bothering to check with them ahead of time about their availability. We don't tell them what the meetings are about. And once we get them into our offices, we sit behind large desks in oversized chairs and seat parents as far away from us as possible. Sometimes we're sarcastic, belligerent, or demeaning. We bring in armies of specialists and support personnel to overwhelm a lone parent, rather than asking ahead of time if there's someone the parent would like to bring along. We feel free to take telephone calls in the middle of a conference or leave parent meetings with no warning. We tell parents rather than ask them. We accuse them rather than listen to them. Here's what one frustrated parent had to say:

> I hate it when school officials say "You must do this for [or with] your child." I'm not a teacher. I have some skills, but teaching is not one of them, and it frustrates me completely when the teacher tries to pin my child's learning failures on me, which, believe me, has frequently happened. After all, the teacher is the expert, right?

Condescension and Rudeness

Parents who are treated rudely and with condescension by educators carry the scars for a long time. They feel demeaned and powerless. Listen to the advice given to administrators by this parent who recently had a serious mad-at-school experience:

> Treat parents as though they have brains in their heads (some of them might just be smarter than some of you). Don't ever be condescending in your responses, and even when you know you're going to have to make an unpopular decision, practice diplomacy and at least hear out the opposition and validate their opinions.

Dishonesty

Principals don't tell outright lies very often, but when they do (usually to cover something inane they did), the parent-principal relationship can be destroyed forever. Little white lies are seductive, but don't be tempted. "Hell hath no fury like a woman scorned," goes the oft-quoted phrase (Congreve, *The Mourning Bride*, act III, scene i). My paraphrase is, "Hell hath no fury like a parent who's been duped."

Sometimes dishonesty comes in the form of just "forgetting" to share some vital information with parents. Families in a Lincoln, Nebraska, school were oblivious to an infestation of brown recluse spiders in the school until a teacher tipped off the community late in the school year. The principal's ostensible reason for keeping the news under his hat: Spiders are nocturnal, so he didn't figure the kids were in danger (Williams, 2004).

Political Correctness to the Max

In an effort to create safe and inviting schools, we educators have banned weapons, drugs, sexual harassment, and profanity, with a vengeance. If questioned about the worth of such policies, most parents would be positive, I'm sure. But can you blame parents for wondering if educators have taken leave of their senses when they suspend a student for having Midol at school or for kissing a classmate on the cheek? By following the letter of the law in their overreaction to fears of being sued, some educators have become the brunt of talk show comedians and newspaper columnists (McElroy, 2003; Riechmann, 1996, p. A4). In a Pittsburgh school where profanity is prohibited in the student code of conduct, a second grader was suspended from school for saying the word "hell." The punishment seems a bit over the top for a seven-year-old who warned a classmate who said "I swear to God," that she would go to hell for taking God's name in vain. Her pronouncement was Biblical but definitely not politically correct. Her father, a police detective, said that his family has a healthy respect for God (World Net Daily, 2004).

Unwillingness to Admit Mistakes and Apologize

Every administrator has done his or her share of dumb things, but parents will usually forgive a mistake, bad judgment, or a momentary lapse of common sense. What they can't abide is unwillingness on the part of the educator to admit the mistake and apologize. I collect ill-advised actions that schools and districts take, and in spite of all of the policies and supervision we have in place, they continue to happen. Several school districts in California, Pennsylvania, and Florida sent out letters to parents of overweight and obese children warning them of the risk factors posed by their conditions. The letters made the news (Galley, 2002; Saunders, 2002), but to date no district personnel have been willing to concede some culpability. As many parents who received the letters pointed out, it isn't the fault of parents that students are served unhealthy school lunches containing more than thirty percent fat; parents have no control over the presence of vending machines that sell high-caloric drinks and snacks in the school cafeteria; and a recent decision to cut physical education classes compounded the problem.

Failure to Give Parents Credit
for Understanding Their Children

Parents would like to have their personal knowledge and understanding of their children validated; they get angry when educators assume that the experts always know best. One parent describes her frustration at being left out of the loop:

> One of the things that bugs me the most about school officials is that they think they know best. Personally, I think the parents usually know best. Officials get hung up sometimes on what they learned in school and start classifying kids. They are so sure a certain method will work with a child and don't bother to ask the parent's opinion.

Lack of Respect for Parents and Children

Administrators are frequently accused of treating parents who are educationally or economically disadvantaged without respect. And that makes the shortchanged parents boil. Administrators talk down to them or take advantage of them in ways they would never dream of doing to the PTA president or a CEO. Assigning the kids of "people who count" to the best teachers, meting out discipline and awards based on parental pressure, and giving perks to a select inside power circle are very demoralizing to the "have-nots." And don't think they aren't aware of exactly what's happening.

Being Asked for Advice and Not Having It Taken

Parents are often invited to be part of local decision-making groups, and they interpret these invitations as a genuine desire on the part of educators for their input. Too often, what educators really want is a rubber stamp process that will allow them to say "we solicited parent input." Parents get angry and feel disenfranchised when the recommendations they make are rearranged or worse yet, ignored.

Unprofessionalism

Administrators draw the ire of parents by doing things such as gossiping, sharing parental confidences, talking derogatorily in public about parents and kids, or looking the other way when teachers are guilty of these same practices.

Reason 3: Education and Educators Fail to Meet Parents' Expectations

Journalist Robert Holland's (1996) book title, *Not With My Child You Don't*, neatly sums up this third category of reasons why parents may be angry, troubled, or afraid: They believe that the schools their children attend are either doing them more harm than good or not doing them any good at all.

Lack of Student Learning, Schoolwide or Districtwide

Although many parents do not understand the debate between the phonics and the whole-language proponents or the difference between process writing and old-fashioned grammar and spelling, they *are* concerned about whether their children will learn to read and write, and they do know when they aren't learning. Being told to "trust us" by educators does nothing to assuage their worries. In fact, an answer like the following response (Ledell & Arnsparger, 1993), given in all sincerity to a question about whether implementing a new curriculum will improve student achievement, can be more disconcerting than reassuring to parents.

> Not conclusively . . . Right now, we don't have reliable ways to measure students' improvements in learning. Traditional standardized tests are inadequate measures of thinking skills, problem-solving abilities, creativity, communication skills, and teamwork. . . . The preliminary indicators of success mentioned earlier [higher graduation rates, better attendance, fewer discipline problems, more students going on to higher education, more comments about improved learning from students and parents], combined with the enthusiastic support of key educators, leading businesses, and many policymakers are sound reasons to have confidence that restructuring will increasingly be recognized as a successful approach to improving student achievement" (p. 20).

Lack of Learning or Behavior Problems Closer to Home

When a child is "falling through the cracks" or being left behind and parents sense that no one at school cares or is even able to respond, they get worried. A mother recently e-mailed me, attracted to my Web site by its focus on reading problems. She and her husband, concerned about their first-grade daughter's lack of reading progress and stonewalled by school personnel, took her to be privately evaluated at a reading clinic where she was diagnosed with a learning disability. They immediately enrolled her in the research-based multisensory reading program at the clinic; she started learning to read immediately. After paying for the extra tutoring for more than a year, the parents finally asked school personnel to take some responsibility. School personnel grudgingly conceded that the child *was* learning disabled but only after redoing all of the tests. They were unwilling, however, to assign a teacher to use the multisensory program in which the child was making progress. Instead, school personnel offered Reading Recovery, an approach very similar to the one used in the classroom that had already proven ineffective.

The frustrated mother wrote to me, "Aren't we entitled to reimbursement from the district for our child's tutoring if they can't provide it within the district? I thought the No Child Left Behind Act was supposed to make sure that all children received what they needed. I know I must sound incredibly naive. I just can't believe that in a school district as wealthy as ours is, with parents who are so interested in their children attending Ivy League schools, that this is what they offer to help her." This parent has just moved from being worried to being downright mad.

Erosion of Values

Many parents are worried that what they hold dear in the areas of morality and decency is being ripped away from them. They watch in dismay as some schools hand out condoms (Berger, 1991) and a middle-school counselor tells parents it's none of their business when she takes their children to a county health clinic to receive birth control pills, Pap smears, and tests for the AIDS virus (Lindsay, 1996).

Pam Angelo, a parent in Antioch, California, objected repeatedly to a required tenth-grade course that asked students personal questions about depression, drugs, grief, and what their parents talk about at home. She didn't ask school officials to change the curriculum, only to have her children excused from the course. To accomplish her goal, she was forced to file a lawsuit. Only after winning the suit was her son finally allowed to enroll in an alternative class ("Lawsuits That Target Schools," 1996).

There is a growing public perception that schools are undermining parental authority and co-opting parental rights (White, 1996). Dana Mack (1997) says, "At the heart of parents' frustration . . . is a deep unbridgeable chasm between the vocabulary of moral dictates, rules, and authority that parents think are best for children and the vocabulary of autonomy and 'choice' that emanates from the classroom" (p. 123).

Lack of Qualified and Competent Teachers

At the bottom of many parental worries about schools is the teaching staff. Parents know that any given school year can be heaven or hell for their child depending on the teacher. Here is one parent's take on teacher competence:

> I have a lot of respect for good teachers. My kids have had some really good ones, with whom I have worked well. They've also had some bad ones, who have been frustrating for me.
>
> Lazy teachers, inept teachers, rude teachers—they run the gamut. When my kids got really good teachers, I would do anything for them. Unfortunately, most of the good ones I've found are in private schools. That's where people work because they love the kids, not money.

The perception that incompetent teachers are protected by unions and receive raises each year simply by staying alive rather than by producing results worries parents. Issues of competence, tenure, and the feeling of powerlessness that overwhelms them when their children have incompetent or uncredentialed teachers cause many parents to become angry with public schools and their administrators.

Lack of Safety

The safety of their children at school continues to be one of the most pervasive worries of parents, and for good reason. The National Center for Education Statistics (2003) reports that seventy-three percent of the U.S. public elementary and secondary schools experienced at least one violent incident during 1999–2000 to include rape, sexual battery other than rape, physical attacks and fights with and without weapons, threats of physical attacks with and without weapons, and robbery with and without weapons, for a total of nearly 1.5 million violent acts (p. vi). In addition to the high-profile and well-publicized incidents of murder and mayhem in schools across the country during the past few years, there are tens of thousands of violent acts that never even make the news. No wonder parents are worried, particularly if they live in urban or high-poverty areas.

Having to Settle for Poor Schools

Financially secure parents can pay their bills and still choose the best public schools or the priciest private schools. But for families who feel they have no choice about their children's education, the fear of having to settle for second-rate schools is real. These parents look at test scores and school finance inequities and know immediately that their children are being cheated out of a quality education by virtue of where they live. Their fears and discontent are driving the voucher and charter schools movements (Peterson, 2003).

Reason 4: Parents Have Personal Problems

A significant number of parents arrive in your office with personal problems that are distressing and often disruptive. Although these problems may not be directly related to their own children, the mission of the school, or education generally, they nonetheless impact the ability of their children to be successful. How can you identify such a parent? Here are the major categories: estranged, separated, and divorced parents; school groupies; complainers, troublemakers, and whiners; abusive parents; and addicted, and dysfunctional, and mentally ill parents.

Estranged, Separated, and Divorced Parents

Consider yourself most fortunate as an administrator if the parents in your school community who are having marital difficulties don't bring their disagreements to school. Most readers have no doubt encountered parents like the noncustodial dad who shared his tale of woe in this letter to the editor of his newspaper:

> I was arrested and spent 12 hours in jail when I attended my son's basketball game. My ex-wife attempted an 'ambush restraining order violation.' Charges were never filed because I provided seven days written notice to her attorney that I would be at the game. My written communications to my son's high school go unanswered. Requests for copies of report cards are ignored. Schools need to make the divorced dad's involvement easier."

This dad's letter was answered shortly thereafter by a school administrator who told her side of the story: Dealing with estranged, separated, and divorced parents is no picnic. She wrote,

As a high school assistant principal and elementary school principal, I have had to catalogue various custody orders, restraining orders and court orders related to divorce and custody decrees. I know kids who have so many warnings stapled to their attendance cards about which parent can take the child on what day that it would make your head swim. I have sat in classrooms on back-to-school night witnessing parents and stepparents giving each other "the eye" and making the lives of teachers miserable.

Stop it. Schools should not be demilitarized zones where children are exchanged like prisoners of war. Schools cannot do the business of schooling if secretaries and administrative staff have to repeatedly be briefed regarding whom they can talk to regarding an absence. Teachers cannot teach if they need a scorecard to keep track of parenting arrangements. When it comes to court appearances, teachers and school personnel should not be dragged in to take sides. In essence, leave the schools out of your wars and battles." (J. Jeffries, personal communication, February 2004).

Most of the parents who fall into this category are able to handle the day-to-day stresses of breaking up a marriage, but the few who can't need special handling to keep their children on track in school.

School Groupies

These parents are on a power trip. Their life is centered in your school, and they won't go home. They want control, information, involvement, and more control. They act like spoiled children, demanding their own way at all costs. In the beginning, school groupies seem supportive and concerned, but just don't cross them or tell them "no." They will harass you, trash you, manipulate you, and are perfectly capable of carrying out a personal vendetta against you that could ruin your career. School groupies are often bright individuals with low self-esteem whose lack of self-confidence and personal worth manifests itself in a desire to make sure that you know who's boss. They often try to take over the parent organization, and many of them run for school boards with personal agendas.

Complainers, Troublemakers, and Whiners

These are parents with multiple axes to grind. They prefer to attack people and not problems. They don't want anyone to do anything that might make things better for them or their children—it's just easier to complain. They don't like anyone, especially themselves. Their children can never please them, either. And you, the educator, will come in for more than your fair share of abuse from these thoroughly disagreeable and unlikable people to whom you are expected to be gracious, warm, and accepting.

Abusive Parents

These parents are abusing their children either psychologically or physically. In cases that are documented, you are legally obligated to report the abuse to the proper authorities, but sometimes the abuse is less obvious and must be confronted in more discreet and subtle ways. Abusive parents sometimes don't feed their children adequately, beat up on them physically and emotionally, seldom come to parent conferences, and can never be reached by phone. But just do or say something they deem inappropriate or prejudicial, and you will find them waiting at your door when you arrive at school.

Addicted, Dysfunctional, and Mentally Ill Parents

These parents consume mountains of time and energy as you attempt to help them and their children. They make promises they don't (or can't) keep, embarrass and humiliate their children, frustrate and clog up the system, lie, and frequently scare you to death with threats, harassment, and verbal abuse. Some are alcoholics, drug addicts, sexual perverts, and criminals. Many have serious mental illnesses. This category of parent is quite rare, but just one can drain your time, energy, and resources.

SUMMING UP AND LOOKING AHEAD

I hope you're not too depressed after reading Chapter 1. The challenges in public education today are enormous, and the need for creative leadership and problem solving is critical. In the face of this onslaught, you must be calm, thoughtful, caring, intelligent, articulate, direct, and honest. In a nutshell, you've got to walk on water *and* leap tall buildings in a single bound. If you feel unprepared to handle the challenges, don't be alarmed. You may need to acquire a new repertoire of behaviors, strategies, and systems. Perhaps dealing with people who are upset comes naturally for you, but most of us need to work hard at keeping our own cool while we're defusing anger, informing the troubled, calming the fearful, and understanding the irrational. The chapters ahead will provide help for you by describing four important steps you can take to deal with difficult parents:

1. Defuse and disarm emotionally charged behavior.

2. Engage in productive problem solving.

3. Create a healthy school culture and climate.

4. Be proactive when it comes to dealing with parents.

Defusing and Disarming Out-of-Control Parents

If you can keep your head when all about you are losing theirs and blaming it on you; If you can trust yourself when all men doubt you, But make allowances for their doubting too; If you can wait and not be tired by waiting, Or, being lied about, don't deal in lies, Or being hated don't give way to hating, And yet don't look too good, nor talk too wise . . .

—Rudyard Kipling (1936)

Learning how to defuse the negative emotions of parents with both real and imagined problems is a critical human relations skill to master. In fact, your effectiveness as an administrator could well depend on your ability to "keep your head when all about you are losing theirs" (Kipling, 1936). Parents who are upset can throw temper tantrums, assault you verbally, or threaten to have you fired. Their feelings are obvious. But don't think for a minute that those parents who are more refined and polite are any less angry. They have just learned how to package their emotions in more appropriate ways. Even though they arrive in Armani suits with polished presentations, their anger is still very real. You can't afford to ignore either group of parents. Although their communication styles and approaches to problem solving may differ, the skills you will need to deal with them remain constant (with a few exceptions).

WHAT IS ANGER?

You no doubt can think of at least one parent who personifies the word *anger* for you. But consider the following definition as a more productive one to help you understand and deal with angry parents. "Anger is an experience that occurs when a goal, value, or expectation that [parents] have chosen has been blocked or when [their] sense of personal worth is threatened" (Taylor & Wilson, 1997, p. 71). Anger can be aroused by both real *and* supposed wrongs. Individuals with irrational and unfounded anger, convinced that everyone in the district is "out to get them," are *paranoid,* and you will never convince them otherwise.

Real anger is an extraordinarily complex emotion that can signal displeasure, hurt, shame, pain, indignation, resentment, exasperation, or annoyance, all of which may range from mild to extreme. The readily identifiable emotional and physiological responses of anger (e.g., a feeling of being cornered, rapid heart beat, red face, loss of control and rational thought) differ from the variety of inappropriate ways in which parents (and their children) express anger. Anger can manifest itself in aggressive behaviors like criticizing, yelling, teasing, ridiculing, or scolding; in physical responses, such as hitting or hurting others; or in more passive ways like silence, withdrawal, or hostile body language (Taylor & Wilson, 1997, pp. 53–54). Hurtful anger that is aggressive or passive-aggressive and seeks to inflict emotional, psychological, or physical damage on another is altogether different from nonhurtful anger that is assertive in nature and seeks to express anger in constructive ways.

Learn to distinguish between the reflexive emotions and physical responses of parents' anger (i.e., when my child or I am threatened, I automatically experience anger) from parents' inappropriate and socially unacceptable ways of *acting out* their anger (e.g., throwing a tantrum or throwing a punch). The emotions of anger cannot be suppressed. The acting out of anger with cruel speech or violent actions (i.e., aggression), or with passive-aggressive responses like the silent treatment or sarcasm, are learned responses that can be unlearned or replaced with more appropriate and productive responses.

HOW TO DEAL WITH PARENTS WHO ARE UPSET OR OUT OF CONTROL

Character Counts

Dealing effectively with angry and out-of-control parents takes character. A principal with high character is an individual whose values, words, and deeds are marked by trustworthiness, integrity, authenticity, respect, generosity, and humility (McEwan, 2003b, p. 134). No one is a paragon of perfection when it comes to character, and "to understand our encounters with difficult people, we eventually need to accept the fact that we are them" (Rosen, 1998, p. 20).

Once we have acknowledged our own character flaws and our tendencies to make the same mistakes our parents do, we must daily aspire to be individuals of high character to whom parents, students, and teachers can look for leadership. With character traits like trustworthiness, integrity, authenticity, and respect on our side, we have "money in the bank" when it comes to dealing with unhappy parents. When we fail, as we ultimately will from time to time, we must be willing to acknowledge and apologize.

Be trustworthy.

You can't make parents trust you. They either do or they don't, based on your behavior, your reputation, or experiences they've had with someone in the same position as yours. Some parents may reserve judgment until they've seen you in action themselves, others will take the word of a friend or neighbor (the grapevine is alive and well), and still others will make up their minds about you immediately, based on nothing more than a gut feeling. Building trust among parents is one of the most important tasks you will undertake as an administrator. Trust is the glue that holds relationships together through tough times. When parents trust you, they give you the benefit of the doubt. They approach you with an attitude of respect that says, "Even though I'm upset with you personally or have questions about the ways things are done here, I know that you're an intelligent, caring person who will try to understand where I'm coming from."

We are not perfect. We have lapses and failures. I remember clearly and with total chagrin the day I lost the trust of one family in my school. I had spent years building the relationship, and I destroyed it in an instant with a carelessly spoken word. The family was a troubled one—three children, each one with unique discipline, learning, and social problems. But we finally got everyone "on the same page" and were making progress. One day, after a particularly frustrating disciplinary encounter with the youngest child, I blew my top in the mail room adjacent to the office. My remarks, inappropriate and unprofessional, were overheard by mom, waiting in the hallway just outside the door. I apologized immediately and profusely, of course, but in just a moment of thoughtless venting, I had destroyed this family's faith in me as an advocate for their children and a trustworthy professional. I learned the hard way that day.

Be honest.

Integrity, the second important trait of character that gives you money in the problem-solving bank, consists of far more than just telling the truth. Integrity speaks of a unity and consistency of personal behavior that withstands scrutiny and invites the confidence of parents. When you are an educator of integrity, you are predictable because you make decisions based on a coherent set of values. You know what you stand for and can articulate your beliefs with eloquence. If you handle problems based on the three P's (politics, pressure, and power), you will soon have a reputation as someone who "blows in the wind," an educator who can be bullied and bought. With that kind of reputation, you can expect more than your fair share of parental problems.

Be authentic.

Authenticity means giving the same kind of attention and respect to everyone regardless of who they are, where they live, what they look like, or how they act. Autry (2001) says, "Be the same person in every circumstance. Hold to the same values in whatever role you have" (p. 10). Authentic principals are consistent, predictable, and utterly transparent. They know who they are and so do the parents whose children attend their schools.

Be respectful.

One doesn't usually think immediately of respect (i.e., consideration, courtesy, and attention) as a correlate of successful schools like effective instruction, standards for learning, and instructional leadership, but in their review of research on effective principals, Persell and Cookson (1982) found "a recurrent characteristic of successful schools concerns the amount of respect shown to all participants" (p. 23). Who better to model and teach respect than the building leader?

Be forgiving.

You may think of forgiveness as a religious concept, and indeed, "Forgiving one who has harmed you liberates you from the emotional prison you have created for yourself . . . [and] is a deeply spiritual act" (Rosen, 1998, p. 255), but forgiveness is also an essential way of being if you intend to remain in the principalship for any length of time. You may think of forgiveness as something you do for someone else, but in reality, it is something you do for yourself. Retaining the slings and darts of angry parents in your psyche is a sure way to lose the vision of why you became an educator in the first place.

The Best Ways to Respond to Angry Parents

> *Those who know don't talk. Those who talk don't know. Close your mouth, block off your senses, Blunt your sharpness, Untie your knots, Soften your glare, Settle your dust.*
>
> —Lao-Tzu (6th century B.C.E./1988, p. 56)

Defusing distressed parents does require a measure of on-the-spot decision making from time to time. However, the more systematic your approach to handling parental concerns can become, the more likely that you will feel confident no matter what or who comes walking through your office door. There are numerous strategies you can routinely use that will help you deal effectively with parents who are upset or even out of control, most of them quite commonsensical. But don't make the mistake of thinking that just because these behaviors sound simple and are the obvious things to do, they will be easy to master. Integrating them into your working life will take time and discipline. You will stumble and fail frequently. These are not behaviors most of us adopt naturally. They demand that we wrestle with our personal values and learn to manage our own emotions. Once you have these strategies firmly established in your own repertoire, however, you will find many problems solving themselves before your very eyes. These strategies fall into three categories: (1) responsive; (2) exploratory; and (3) action (The terms *exploratory* and *action* are adapted from Kottler & McEwan [1999]). We discuss the responsive strategies in this chapter and tackle the exploratory and action strategies in Chapter 3.

As you consider how best to integrate these three types of strategies into your personal communication style, remember that disarming hostile and frustrated parents is an art, not a science. In the beginning, choose a single strategy that you find difficult to use automatically and practice it with everyone you talk to. For me personally, listening intently without becoming distracted or losing focus was my first goal. You may have to work on being less defensive or monitoring your body language so that it doesn't exacerbate an already explosive situation.

A rule of thumb when working with angry parents is to use the strategies in a somewhat sequential fashion: (1) respond, (2) explore, and (3) act. However, every individual or couple is different. With some parents, the process may only take one meeting; with others, it may take months (or even years). That is the art of working with difficult parents—knowing, as the country western song goes, "when to hold and when to fold."

The ancient wisdom of Lao-Tzu found in the epigraph sums up the essence of being responsive. During this initial stage of meeting with an angry parent, don't ask questions or gather information; that comes later during the exploratory stage. Don't set goals, attempt to solve the problem, or tell parents what actions you will take. Save "leaping tall buildings in a single bound" for later. The responsive stage is all about closing your mouth, untying your knots, and softening your glare. As Lao-Tzu advises, Settle your dust (in a chair pulled alongside a parent) and close your mouth.

Manage by walking around.

There is no substitute for knowledge when dealing with angry parents. Knowing the backgrounds of each of the families in your school isn't always possible, but understanding where a distressed parent is coming from can often turn confrontation into collaboration and keep a conflict from becoming a conflagration.

What is the best way to acquire knowledge? Go to all of the prereferral meetings, staffings, and problem-solving meetings that are held in your school. Visit every classroom every day and take note of students who appear to be having difficulties academically or behaviorally. Talk with their teachers. Learn the names of students (and their siblings and their parents). Visit the cafeteria, music class, the library, the gym, and the art room. Go out for recess once in awhile. Eat lunch with students. Hang out in the faculty lounge occasionally. Talk to bus drivers, cafeteria personnel, and the custodian. Being an effective administrator is a lot like being an intelligence agent. Information is power. When parents share their versions of what happened in a classroom or on the playground (according to their child), if you were there, you can set them straight. Someone gave me some advice when I was a new administrator: "Be all over your building like a rash." It was a unique way of communicating a key principle of instructional leadership: Be a visible presence. Some call it management by walking around.

Assume problems.

If parents make an appointment to meet with the principal, assume they have some kind of problem to discuss with you. So don't immediately take over the conversation in such a way that they feel powerless to interrupt or change the subject. Rather, send the message that you are eager to have them share their concerns and that you do indeed invite them to bring up a problem.

Don't delegate.

You may be tempted to hide in your office when you hear trouble coming down the hallway, especially if you have a secretary who is both willing and able to handle touchy situations. As attractive as this option may seem, don't dodge trouble. Oh, it's wonderful to have a silver-tongued secretary who can calm troubled waters, but save her as a backup for when you're out of the building. Parents (and teachers) will soon catch on to your game if you regularly hide from conflict, and they won't like it one bit. Furthermore, you will be thought of as a figurehead who can't or won't do the hard stuff, and your credibility will disappear. In addition, your secretary will soon assume that she's in charge, and while you should be delighted to have an ambitious and talented secretary who can fill in during emergencies, if you count on her to do it all, she will soon start telling you how to do your job.

Welcome and accept.

Shake hands and welcome parents into your office. Even the most hostile parents will usually warm up to a personal greeting and a welcoming touch, if appropriate. Sit eye to eye and knee to knee. This practice is a key principle of group dynamics. It means that people need proximity to one another to connect. When people are seated too far away from one another, the space between them inhibits communication. Don't sit behind your desk when meeting with parents. Sit side by side at a round table that could include other participants if needed. Provide comfortable chairs and offer coffee, water, or a soft drink, if available, to put parents at ease.

Say something nice.

Share a compliment about the child in question with the parents. If possible, do your homework before the meeting. Look at the student's cumulative folder and consult with specialists to determine any unique talents. One genuine compliment will help to set a positive tone for the conference. Remember what your mother always said, "If you can't say something nice about somebody, don't say anything at all."

Self-neutralize.

Sandra Crowe (1999) suggests that the first thing you do when confronted with difficult people is to self-neutralize; that is, repeat to yourself, "This isn't personal. It's not about me" (p. 121).

And most of the time it isn't about you. It's about teachers, curricula, policies, and discipline procedures. When it isn't about "real" problems, it's usually about the parents' inability to accept the notion that someone else is in charge of their most precious possessions, their children.

Remaining neutral does not mean you lack empathy or have a dispassionate attitude toward parents who are distressed. It means that you should not feel responsible or take ownership of an angry parent's feelings and behavior. If parents are angry, upset, and troubled, it's not your fault. (Of course, if you really have blown it, by all means apologize and move on.) Do all you can do to defuse their anger, but then relax, put it aside, and sleep soundly that night. Don't let parents' anxiety, frustration, and hostility consume your energies and demoralize your own emotional state.

Attend.

Being attentive to parents who are distressed is essential. Attending means giving people your undivided interest. It means using your body, your face, and especially your eyes, to say, "Nothing exists right now for me except you. Every ounce of my energy and being is focused on you."

This kind of intense concentration calls for structuring one-on-one time with parents in an atmosphere that is free from interruptions. Clear away clutter. Remove anything that might interfere with your focus. Turn off the telephones and shut the door. I lowered the blinds on the window in my door unless I was meeting with a highly charged and possibly dangerous parent. Our office "complex" was very small, and everyone (parents, teachers, and even students) loved to look into my windows to see who was on the hot seat or what I was doing. Not only did these smiling faces at the window distract me; they made any visitors to my office feel as though they were in a fish bowl.

Angry parents, in particular, are often so used to being devalued by others that attending behaviors instantly tell them something is different about this interaction: "Here is a person who seems to care about me and what I have to say." But all adults in today's fast-track world will find having the full attention of an "important" person like the principal a somewhat rare and enormously affirming experience.

Listen.

An important part of true listening is a mental exercise called *bracketing*, the temporary giving up or setting aside of one's own assumptions and prejudices, to experience as far as possible the speaker's world from the inside (Peck, 1978, p. 73). The first thing to do when a parent with a problem comes to call is to listen. I personally have always had a very hard time listening. Impulsive and easily distracted, my mind has "a mind of its own." It could be wandering elsewhere, planning dinner, or making up a to-do list; I might be thinking of what I want to say in response or formulating the perfect solution to the problem being presented. I've learned the hard way that none of these approaches wins friends, influences people, *or* solves problems. Because I am also hearing impaired, I must overcome yet another set of challenges to effective listening. Men with mustaches and accents are my nemesis. If I lose the main idea, recovering it without appearing inept is difficult. I've also discovered that listening is a whole lot more than just hearing the words people are speaking. Their facial expressions, body language, and tone of voice can communicate volumes about their true feelings.

Be gentle.

Gentleness and artfulness are among the most effective ways of defusing anger while at the same time giving you the opportunity to determine the real source of the anger (Taylor & Wilson, 1997, p. 67). Gentleness connotes courtesy, refinement, serenity, civility, and patience. If you have an assertive and strong personality, cultivating gentleness may seem to be an artifice. But you will be amazed to see how "a soft answer [can] turn away wrath, [whereas] a harsh word stirs up anger" (Proverbs 15:1, Revised Standard Version). The term *artfulness* suggests cleverness and skill, a talent you have cultivated and worked on. Believe me, being gentle in the face of a parent gone ballistic doesn't feel normal when you first try it. Defending, excusing, and accusing come far more readily to the surface of our feelings and actions.

The tone and quality of your voice are just as important as the words you speak. If you are hurried, hostile, defensive, or distracted, your voice will give you away immediately, and parents will judge you to be insincere, even if you are saying all the right things. A soft answer means that you don't contradict, correct, condescend, or disagree with parents who are already infuriated, even if they are misinformed. Don't be impatient or act harried. At first, this may take a will of steel.

Read between the lines.

Management consultant Peter Drucker (2004) writes, "The most important thing in communication is hearing what isn't said." Infer and intuit. Sometimes people don't have the courage to say what they need or want to say. If you can decipher their intent and feed it back to them for confirmation, you can ease parents' fears and concerns without their having to fully articulate them. This is a tricky strategy and must be used with discretion.

Give "wordless advice."

It has taken me years of practice to perfect the art of giving what I call wordless advice, not only with parents who are upset but with my own family members. I finally learned that when people come to me with a problem, they don't necessarily want my advice, they just want an empathetic ear. They don't want my eyes to glaze over and my mind to drift to personal agendas; they want my full attention and thoughtful nods and "hmms." They don't want me to talk "at" them, either. They need a sounding board, a place to reason out their own problems. By the time they finish their monologues, they thank me for the great advice (I never said a word) and go merrily on their ways. Here's a summary of what you can do to become a better listener:

Notice the attitudes and feelings of individuals. They may communicate something different from what the words are saying. Posture, eye movements, hand gestures, tone of voice, and facial expressions are powerful communicators.

Listen between the lines for what a parent is *not* saying in addition to what is being said.

Do not respond with your own message by evaluating, sympathizing, giving your opinion, offering advice, analyzing, or questioning. Simply report back what you heard in the message as well as the attitudes and the feelings that were expressed.

Make occasional and appropriate verbal responses, such as "Oh," "Hmm," or "Uh-huh," to confirm to the speaker that you are paying attention. Parents need to feel that you are understanding them both emotionally (e.g., their feelings of anger or fear) and intellectually (the actual words they are saying).

Keep listening until there is a sign that the speaker has finished speaking and is ready to listen to you.

If appropriate to the specific situation and not upsetting to the parents, take notes to help you remember critical details of the conversation. Most parents with problems will be relieved to know that someone is finally listening to them and cares enough to write it down. Taking notes can help you to focus more readily, *and* sometimes taking notes helps parents to take more care with what they say.

Convey serenity.

Convey serenity with body language that is calm and receptive. Maintain eye contact, sit quietly without fidgeting, and arrange your hands and arms in a nonthreatening way—uncrossed and relaxed. Don't frown, grimace, sigh, play with your hair, crack your knuckles, tap your fingers, yawn, adjust your clothing, roll your eyes, slouch your body, grit your teeth, chew gum, cross and uncross your legs, move too quickly, look alarmed, or make faces. Nod your head occasionally to indicate you understand the speaker. Remain attentive without appearing tense or threatened.

Be a mirror.

Give support and encouragement to parents who are distressed, by "be[ing] a clean mirror, [neither] descriptive . . . interpretive nor judgmental" (Wegela, 1996, p. 160). Rather than judging or interpreting what parents are saying, hold up a mirror so they can see what their behavior may be doing to their children, to the teachers, or to themselves. Describe what you see happening, *not* how you feel about it.

Backtrack.

Backtracking is a form of feedback in which you repeat back *some* of the same words or phrases that another person is using (Brinkman & Kirschner, 1994, p. 45). Although paraphrasing (different from backtracking) is often recommended as a way of confirming that you have understood what someone is saying, perceptive people often resent having their words replaced by your words. To them, that implies that you're twisting the meaning of what they've said. In backtracking, you don't echo everything that is said but instead, focus on key words that capture the main idea. This will let parents know that you have heard and understood their concerns. For example, if Mr. Marsh is upset about the reading curriculum being used in his son's second grade, believing that it is not based on solid scientific research, you might backtrack with Mr. Marsh using the following statement: "Mr. Marsh, if I understand you correctly, you're looking for some solid experimental research that the reading program we've chosen gets results."

Open your mind.

Parents who are troubled and frightened often need permission and acceptance from administrators to share their private and deeply felt concerns. If they sense that an educator isn't interested, doesn't care, or is passing premature judgment, they may well get cold feet and leave without articulating the real problem. Parents need the freedom to explore an issue without criticism or censure. In the process, you may be exposed to a new point of view or an alternative way of viewing education, so suspend your initial prejudice or distaste and become a learner.

Don't react.

Reacting is acting without thinking. There are many possible ways to react that are inappropriate. Sometimes, our first inclination when cornered by an angry parent is to strike back (e.g., counterattack, defend, explain, justify, or just plain cut off and "divorce" parents we don't like). Instead, step back and remain neutral. Don't personalize the attack and try to convince the parent of their wrongness and your rightness. Equally ineffective is giving in just to get a parent out of your office *and* your life, without regard for the child, any teachers who may be involved, or policies already in place to handle such situations. Be firm and stand your ground while solving problems. Having a reputation as a wimpy pushover is almost as bad as being labeled a terrible tyrant. Command respect: Neither run away from the problem nor gear up for battle.

Remain composed.

"To change a difficult person, you must first change yourself—your way of thinking about the person and your way of responding to the familiar provocations" (Tavris, 1978, p. 294). Most of us find it difficult to be neutral about parents who are angry and hostile. They bring out the worst in us. Maintaining your composure will effectively dismantle the hostile feedback loop that can be created if you respond in kind to angry words. As Tavris goes on to say,

> If you're pleasant and cordial, you will, in the long run, wear them down, even get them to be cordial back. It's surprising how often they warm up—not always, but often—because so often their hostility masks their own loneliness and insecurity. And in the long run, who benefits most by your being friendly and cordial? You do. (p. 299)

Your composure and courtesy will act as a mirror in which parents will find their own desperate attempts to intimidate and abuse embarrassingly and unattractively reflected. When parents sense your confidence, and they will, their bluster and bravado will diminish. If they sense fear and uncertainty, they will take advantage of it every time.

Be assertive.

Inward feelings of negativity and low self-esteem can make it very difficult for principals to handle angry parents. Cultivating positive feelings of self-esteem will enable you to manage your own anger more effectively as well as to place angry parents' feelings in perspective. Angry and hostile parents are a little like dogs and horses. They sense when you are unsure or hesitant and will take over before you know it.

Here in Arizona where I live, mountain lions are not uncommon. A leaflet distributed by the National Park Service advises hikers and campers to do the following if they meet a mountain lion: "Always give them a way to escape. Don't run. Stay calm. Hold your ground, or back away slowly. Face the lion and stand upright. Do all you can to appear larger. Grab a stick. Raise your arms. If you have small children with you, pick them up. . . . The goal is to convince it that you are not prey and may be dangerous yourself. If attacked, fight back!" (Wildlife Hazards, 2004). These suggestions may seem somewhat humorous or even outrageous when applied to angry parents, but there are some lessons to be learned here. Be confident. Don't let angry parents back you into a corner or scare you. Stand tall and do all you can to appear in charge, in control, and willing to stand your ground.

Administer shock therapy.

If you are personally being browbeaten and bullied by a parent, stop the parent in his or her tracks immediately with a firm assertion: "Mr. Flint, I can understand why you are so distressed. I would like to talk with you about how your child is being treated and make sure that it doesn't happen again. But first you have to sit down, lower your voice, and stop swearing. At ABC School we always try to treat one another with respect. That's why we're not going to tolerate someone being rude to your son on the play-ground, and I can't tolerate rude behavior from you, either. So please calm down, and let's begin all over again." Administering this kind of shock therapy can remind parents where they are, with whom they are speaking, and what their real priority is—their child (Axelrod & Holtje, 1997, p. 87).

Take the A train.

Perhaps the thought of taking the A train stirs memories of your first subway trip in New York City. Or if you're fond of big band music, you might think immediately of Duke Ellington's classic. But for dealing with angry people, customers in particular, Sam Horn (1996, p. 32) suggests a different kind of A train, one that takes you and an angry individual to a more expeditious resolution of a problem: Agree, apologize, act, and appreciate. The A train works just as well with angry parents as it does with angry customers. These behaviors can be used singly or in any combination, but they are all extraordinarily powerful because angry parents don't expect them. Accepting and affirming the fact that people are upset and may well have a perfectly logical and justifiable reason for feeling the way they do doesn't mean that you approve the manner in which they are seeking to address their anger or grievance, and it's acceptable to communicate that concept to an angry parent. Being willing and able to accept the reality of their anger (or agree that they do indeed have a reason to be angry) is an important first step toward solving the problem that stirred up the hornet's nest in the first place.

Apologize.

Sometimes, the first words from your mouth should be an apology, when a parent stops talking long enough to come up for air. In these litigious days, many of us educators are loathe to say we are sorry, fearing lawsuits and damages, but not saying you're sorry when you are obviously at fault will only exacerbate an already difficult situation. Often, if we are willing to apologize, parents will back down and admit that they or their child are also at fault. When my daughter was in high school, one of her favorite teachers called her a "bitch." Both she and I were understandably dismayed. I asked the principal to arrange a meeting for us with the teacher, the outcome of which I hoped would be a simple apology and an admission that a mistake had been made. That's all we wanted. If it had not been forthcoming, I can only imagine how much time and energy I might have expended on righting the wrong. But the teacher *and* the principal apologized. My daughter was able to ask the teacher for a college recommendation, and everyone lived happily ever after. Except the teacher. He continued to make this same mistake over and over again. He was ultimately dismissed for sexual harassment, among other errors in judgment. But that's another story.

Empathize.

Learn to lay aside your own needs to be heard and understood and instead focus on hearing and understanding what parents have to say. Perhaps you have never had an experience identical to the one they are having, but suspend disbelief for a moment and imagine yourself in the parents' shoes. How would you feel? How would you act? Where would you go for help? Suppose your child was being evaluated for mental retardation. Would you be calm, trusting, and totally relaxed? I doubt it. Suppose your child was being bullied on the playground, and you thought no one cared. Would you take it lying down? Probably not. If you sincerely engage in this exercise of imagination, the parents with whom you are meeting will feel your empathy and begin to relax. I shudder with embarrassment when I think of a parent-teacher conference I had early in my teaching career. I had the temerity to suggest to the mother of nine children that she should spend at least thirty minutes every school night helping her fifth grade son master his multiplication facts. I still remember the look of utter amazement she gave me. As a brand-new teacher I was long on enthusiasm but very short on empathy.

Welcome criticism.

To welcome criticism is to take the "Appreciate" car on the "A" Train. Perhaps the idea of welcoming criticism from parents or being appreciative for the bad news they bear is as attractive to you as the prospect of oral surgery. But sometimes we need to hear and heed what parents have to say that might help us improve how we deliver education to their children. And even when the criticism is more destructive than constructive, we need to listen and respond with openness, interest, and appreciation. John Foster Dulles (2004), the noted statesman, once said, "The measure of success is not whether you have a tough problem to deal with, but whether it is the same problem you had last year." If you have a steady stream of distressed parents complaining about the same issue (e.g., conditions in the lunchroom, unsafe playground equipment, an abusive bus driver), it's time to address these issues and stop burying your head in the sand. The worst thing you can ever say to a parent who comes to you with a concern is, "You're the only person who's ever complained about this." Even if the statement is true, it won't be for long when they get home and start phoning everyone on the class list.

If there's a problem, tell parents you'll investigate it and thank them for bringing it to your attention. Then, start investigating.

Consider cultural differences.

When the parents with whom you are meeting have a different cultural background than you do, try to understand the subtleties that characterize their nonverbal behaviors and communication patterns. Nonverbal signals to consider include distance between people, eye contact, and whether touching is expected or appropriate. Who should initiate the conversation, whether interrupting is acceptable, and how to bring up difficult topics are also important considerations. If you are aware of cultural differences, you can alter your behavior patterns to put parents at ease and increase the likelihood of productive problem solving.

If you are working with a translator, never address your remarks to the translator. He or she is merely a conduit. Maintain eye contact with the parents. Learn how to say hello, good-bye, thank you for coming, and I'll do all I can to help you in several languages if necessary.

End positively.

At the close of the conference, summarize what you think you've heard. Not only is this a good-faith gesture that lets parents know you fully understand their point of view, but a brief review of critical information will clear up any misconceptions that may exist on either side of the table. Even if the meeting concludes without con-sensus, the knowledge that they have been heard and understood will defuse most angry parents and calm the most anxious ones. Be sure to keep careful notes of the action items for immediate follow-up.

STRATEGIES FOR DEALING WITH TRULY TROUBLED PARENTS

I wish I could promise you a money-back guarantee for any instances that the aforementioned responsive strategies don't pro-duce positive feedback from all parents. But if you have tried every approach you can think of and the storm clouds are still hovering, then it is likely you have encountered one of a small but challenging group of parents that make even the most self-confident educators shiver in their shoes. I have yet to meet the educator who doesn't instantly resonate with my choice of the term "crazy" to describe *some* of the parents who fall into one or more of the following categories. Their outrageous behavior often requires special handling!

Estranged, Separated, and Divorced Parents

If perfectly normal parents start acting erratic and irresponsible, consider the possibility that their marriage is in trouble. Of course you must keep your speculations to yourself, but as the old pop song goes, "breaking up is hard to do." I am certainly not suggesting that every couple that decides to end their marriage will require hand-holding by the principal. Thankfully, most adults handle their private lives in private. But many couples seem to break up with hostility, anger, temper tantrums, and even physical violence and damage to property. The minute the news *is* public, it's important for school personnel to be in the know—not as to who did what and when to whom, but to have a record of what types of custody agreements are in place, where children will be living and when, whether grandparents are involved, where to reach parents in case of emergencies, and whether any restraining orders have been issued by a judge. Principals *must* do the legal thing. Unfortunately, the legal thing doesn't always seem to make sense, but ours is not to reason why. Don't get too cozy with either mom or dad, or you could find yourself triangulated in a divorce case and be subpoenaed to testify. Offer a listening ear and counsel regarding the child's academic, behavioral, and social problems at school. Your role is to ensure that children feel secure and safe at school. Politely decline to hear the particulars of a family's marital woes.

Parents on Power Trips

Parents on a power trip are in a special category all by themselves. Often their children are gentle and very cooperative, because when one of your parents is on a power trip, you want to be seen and not heard. Parents on power trips remind me of construction equipment: Jackhammers, dump trucks, and bulldozers seem very apropos to illustrate the critical attributes of parents on power trips. They want to take over the PTA and tell you how to run your school. They are arrogant and will fill any power vacuum that exists, especially one in the principal's office. Once you have tried attending, listening, and empathizing, you may need to take a page from one highly effective principal I know who has no trouble banning parents politely but firmly when they assert themselves inappropriately.

Bulldozers

Parents disguised as bulldozers come rolling into your office ready to run over and flatten anybody in their vicinity. They are loud, hostile, and can do a great deal of damage in a short period of time. However, many of the strategies we described earlier work very well with bulldozers. Listen and let them tell their stories. If you need to interrupt to get them to sit down and stop swearing, do so. Remember the tricks that hikers are advised to use on mountain lions. They actually work well with bulldozers. Look them right in the eye and make yourself look big and powerful. Be firm and forceful, but not hostile or demeaning. Don't talk to a bulldozer as you would to a child. Talk to a bulldozer as if you were a slightly bigger bulldozer. My experience with bulldozers is that once you demonstrate your ability to listen, your refusal to take any nonsense, and your willingness to solve genuine problems, they will be your lifelong supporters. Most of their bluster and bravado is based on a perceived inability to get people to listen to them. When you show them respect (once they calm down), they will turn into kitty cats.

Jackhammers

Jackhammer parents never come into your office with their hammers up and running. That would be far too obvious. Instead, they operate undercover, breaking up what you believed were solid relationships and effectively destroying your school's culture and climate with just a few jabs and thrusts of their vibrating rotors. The most effective strategy to use with jackhammers is to bring them out into the open so that other folks can hear and see the damage they are doing. Confront their behavior in quiet but forceful ways. If they are sarcastic and playful with their damaging comments in front of an audience, call them on their behavior. Jackhammers often do their "best" work in meetings where they are counting on you to let their inappropriate behavior pass.

If Mr. Thompson starts making snide and sarcastic remarks at the PTA Board meeting about the number of newspaper articles featuring another school in the district, be ready for him. "Are you saying that we're doing a poor job with publicity, Mr. Thompson?" His statement may well be a slam on your ability to get the job done, or he doesn't really know how to go about getting what he wants—more positive publicity for the school. But his behavior clearly signals a need to bring his concerns out in the open. Don't let Mr. Thompson get away with ripping you up one side and down the other, all the while pretending to be "nice."

Dump trucks

Dump truck dads and moms are often acting out a more grown-up version of a toddler's temper tantrum. You never know what's going to set them off. Maybe they missed their nap. Or it could just be the barometric pressure. Who knows? In most cases, a parent who dumps a load of garbage at your office door actually feels threatened or powerless. You can't always predict when a delivery of "dirt" may occur, but just know that it wasn't anything *you* said or did. If parents are having tantrums, your first goal is to get them calmed down. Sometimes that takes raising your voice several decibels to get through the haze of hostility. If you're meeting with a parent and you feel a tantrum coming on, stand up, grip the table, and say, "Let's stop right here for a second. I have an idea that might work." The sudden interruption may shock the parent enough to forestall the tantrum. Take the tantrum seriously and try to address the underlying issue or problem in a productive way once the parent has regained control.

Complainers

Parents who whine and complain aren't as scary as the parents on a power trip or the aggressive types who lose control in your office, but they do have a way of wearing you down, particularly those of you who want to be helpful and keep their schools running smoothly. Parents who have genuine problems to solve are relatively easy to handle—find out what the problem is, gather information about possible solutions (either alone or with a team), put forth some possible solutions, and choose the best one to implement. Cross it off your list.

The big problem with complainers is that they rarely have a *real* problem to attack. Oh, they know how to put their fingers on problems, but they are impossible to get a handle on—like Jell-o. For example, there's Mrs. MacArthur who whines incessantly about her bus problems. Granted, the stop is not in the most convenient location for her (she can't see it from her front window); granted, the driver is a little brusque at times (dealing with Mrs. MacArthur every morning at 6:45 a.m. can do that to you); and granted, the bus drop off time isn't always firm (construction traffic is the current problem). However, when you take a close look at Mrs. MacArthur's problems, there's not a single solitary thing you can do to change anything. The bus stop has been there for twenty-five years. Just because Mrs. MacArthur doesn't like it, it's not going to get moved. The bus driver, while not a charm school graduate, has never raised his voice or used profanity with Mrs. MacArthur. He treats her just like he treats his whining wife—he ignores her. Construction is a fact of life and traffic jams are not under the control of school principals. So what do you do with Mrs. MacArthur?

In the first place, recognize that she sees the world through a different set of glasses than the majority of parents in your school. She feels powerless, is prescriptive about the way things *should* be, and is convinced that she is perfect (Bramson, 1982, p. 41). Mrs. MacArthur feels powerless to make anything happen in her life and needs somebody powerful to help her. She believes that things ought to be a certain way and it bugs her no end when they aren't. She needs someone to change things for her. Last, Mrs. MacArthur knows that if she is going to cover up for the fact that she is not perfection personified, she has to constantly find others to blame for whatever is making her unhappy. "[Complainers'] sense of powerlessness creates a vacuum that sucks in [principals] who have a strong wish to help others" (p. 43).

You can deal with complainers by using some of the strategies described earlier in the chapter: Listen. Acknowledge that you do understand where Mrs. MacArthur is coming from. The bus stop might not be in the most convenient place for *her.* But don't ever take responsibility for that. Now if her son's life were in danger because of reckless bus driving or the bus driver had said or done something obscene to either her or her son, it *would* be your problem. But construction traffic, the taciturn manner of the bus driver, and the fact that she has to cross the street to meet the bus are not *your* problems.

Continually reiterate the facts of the case to keep yourself from being sucked into Mrs. MacArthur's little game: The bus stop is not going to be changed. The bus driver's iconoclastic personality is not grounds for his dismissal. Construction traffic is unavoidable and until the James Street overpass is completed, the bus may run a few minutes late on some afternoons. Suggest that if Mrs. MacArthur still has problems with this issue that she write a letter to the business manager or the board of education or the newspaper. Accept the fact that neither you nor anyone else will ever make Mrs. MacArthur a happy camper. But always listen to what she has to say, because you never know when she *will* identify a genuine problem.

Abusive, Addictive, Violent, and Mentally Ill Parents

This category of parents needs *very* special handling *and* as much professional assistance as you have available. Here are the must-do's when dealing with abusive, addictive, violent, or mentally ill parents.

1. Gather as much information as you can about the parents to help you understand their behavior and motivations.

2. Make sure that you follow all of the rules when dealing with parents who live on the edge. The fact that parents are breaking the rules left and right should never tempt you to play their game.

3. Although you might suspect that parents are abusing drugs or alcohol, never accuse them. Call the police if you have any suspicions and let them handle the situation. If possible, keep your office doors open and alert office personnel to a possible need for a 911 call.

4. Watch for physical signs of impending violence, such as clenched fists, agitated tone of voice, flared nostrils, red face, and wide-open eyes (Morgan, 2003, p. 44). If you have any reason to believe parents are carrying weapons, call the police immediately and have an emergency plan in place to evacuate the hallways and lock down the classrooms.

5. Keep careful and complete notes about all experiences and encounters with this category of parents. If you don't write it all down, later you may doubt that it ever happened. But more important, parents may begin to lie or contradict your version, and you will need records of what was said and when. In some cases, you might even need a witness to confirm that a letter was sent or a document delivered to parents.

6. Keep superiors informed. One of my least favorite memories is of Mrs. Swanson. She was about to deliver her sixth child, and she had the three who weren't yet enrolled in school in tow when she exploded into my office with a problem. The techniques that usually worked with so-called normal parents were useless; she was out of control. "If you can't help me, I'll find somebody who will," she screamed, as she dragged her entourage of runny noses and unchanged diapers down the hall. I picked up the phone to let the superintendent know that a storm front was heading his way. It was a good thing. Five minutes later, the whole crew was sitting in his outer office refusing to budge until he gave them an audience. I was able to give my synopsis of the situation and explain what I had already done to try to solve the problem. Never underestimate the power of an irrational and out-of-control parent to wreak havoc. Get there first with the facts. Keep central office informed. They will appreciate your early warning system.

7. Consult with mental health professionals. If you are dealing with a parent who has shared a medical diagnosis with you (e.g., bipolar disorder or depression), learn more about it so you don't thoughtlessly say or do the wrong thing.

8. Consult with law enforcement officials in advance of a meeting, if possible. There have been occasions when I have asked for a police officer to be available in the school building during a conference with a potentially dangerous parent. You must protect your own safety and that of your staff members.

9. Know your school board policies and the legal rights of parents and students as well as the requirements of your own job description. There will be parents who have read all of these documents and be waiting to trap you.

10. Invite someone else to attend the parent conference to take notes or to witness what is happening. Use the special skills of the counselor, social worker, or school psychologist to help you defuse an explosive situation.

11. Be aware of the laws protecting the rights of children and your legal obligation to report any abuse of the children who attend your school.

12. Find a trusted colleague or superior with whom to discuss the problem and how you are handling it. Don't go it alone. Ask them for advice and perspective and then be prepared to follow through on their suggestions if they will help resolve the situation. Take care, however, to be discreet. The more individuals with whom you share your story, the more likely it will find its way back to the wrong person.

13. Don't take it personally. It may seem at times as though an out-of-control parent's behavior is targeted specifically at you. However, if you have an opportunity to talk with the teachers or administrator at a formerly attended school, you will no doubt find similar behavior patterns.

14. Make sure that you know how to handle your own emotions or you can make a difficult situation impossible.

15. Be aware of the rights you have to ban disruptive, dysfunctional, and dangerous parents from your school property. Consult with your superintendent to determine the precise procedures to follow.

USING YOUR ENCOUNTERS WITH PARENTS TO LEARN AND GROW

Buddhists believe that we can and should be grateful for everyone who crosses our path. That point of view is a difficult one to embrace when we've just been raked over the coals by an irate parent. Why should we be grateful for someone who's out to make our life miserable? Or so it seems. But if you look on each encounter with a parent who's angry, troubled, afraid, or out of control psychologically or behaviorally as an opportunity to learn and grow as a person and professional, you will find yourself developing an entirely different attitude about dealing with challenging and difficult parents. Sometimes, in the midst of the harsh words and angry tempers, you will learn patience and forbearance. Often, while you're enduring frustration and embarrassment, you will reach deep within and discover a gift for helping others to solve seemingly insoluble problems. You will learn to manage and channel your own feelings of anger and fear, and in your strength, be a resource to parents who need wise counsel more than ever. In the end, however, we do it for the children.

SUMMING UP AND LOOKING AHEAD

In Chapter 1 we explored some of the reasons that parents may be angry and troubled with what's happening at school, and in this chapter we have examined a variety of responsive strategies to defuse and disarm the mildly upset as well as the over-the-edge parents who show up at your office door. Just ahead, in Chapter 3 we will describe the most common types of problem situations found in schools and suggest some exploratory and action strategies to solve them and gradually begin to reduce the number of angry-parent encounters you have during the course of a school year.

Solving the Problems That Make Parents Angry, Troubled, Afraid, or Just Plain Crazy

The mere formulation of a problem is often far more essential than its solution.

—Albert Einstein

Defusing and disarming the emotionally charged parents who arrive on your doorstep is only the first step. Once a *real* problem is identified and agreed on, it's time to use the exploratory and action strategies found in this chapter to help solve the problem that created parents' anger, fear, and distress in the first place. I do hope that you love problems if you have chosen a career in education, for if you don't, you no doubt face a measure of trepidation each day, wondering when you'll receive the next phone call or visit from a distressed parent. But don't ever let the members of your school community (staff members, parents, or students) get the feeling that you don't want to hear bad news. Soon, everyone but you will know "the sky is falling." If you are guilty of any of the following behaviors, become more receptive and open to hearing about potential problems and difficult situations. Forewarned is forearmed.

- Do you subtly discourage people from rocking the boat or bringing bad news to your attention?
- Do you avoid asking open-ended questions of parents, students, and teachers, such as "How are things going?" or "Are you feeling good about school this year?" for fear that you might get an answer you won't like?
- Do you purposely focus on administrivia so that you are too busy to handle problems?
- Do you delegate angry parents to your secretary because she seems so capable?
- Do you keep your schedule so tightly structured that you are protected from the real world in your school, which is teeming with problems of every kind?
- Do you wear blinders when you walk down your hallways and visit the classrooms of your school?

THE PERVASIVE PROBLEMS THAT PLAGUE US

School problems come in all shapes and sizes. They occur in the classroom, on the playground, in the lunchroom, and on the bus. Sometimes, students notice them first, or parents call the principal with a concern. But more often than not, educators identify the problems at school and then have to decide how best to resolve them. School problems that are ignored or left unsolved can result in unhappy parents, and when parents are upset, chances are their children will be doing less than their best in school.

For purposes of this discussion, a school problem is defined as anything that keeps a child from achieving his or her learning potential. Sometimes, school problems can be solved with a phone call or a brief parent-teacher conference. Sometimes, a long-term, comprehensive intervention plan is needed. But if ignored, a real school problem can grow like an out-of-control weed, choking communication between home and school, cutting off trust and cooperation, and stifling the academic growth of the student. Let's look at the three major sources of school problems in more detail.

Problems Identified by School Personnel

Educators specialize in identifying problems, although I've often felt like we're much better at finding them than at solving them. Skilled teachers can often identify several children with problems before the first week of school is over. The best teachers give children some time to settle in, do what they can to solve a problem at school, and then notify parents if all is not well.

The concern may come in the form of a telephone call, a handwritten note, or a formal report card. The phrases are usually polite and couched in educational jargon, but the meaning is quite clear to parents: "Your child isn't measuring up to some standard of behavior or achievement and you need to do something about it."

"Mary seems a bit immature with regard to her social relationships."

"I'm concerned about John's behavior. He isn't following our classroom rules, and none of my usual strategies seem to be working."

"Sarah is falling behind in her work. She has failed the last two math tests, and if she doesn't spend more time studying for the next quiz, she might receive a failing grade."

"Your daughter can't seem to get along with anyone. She wants her own way no matter what the situation."

"We're concerned about a possible learning problem with your son, Jeremy. Could you call and make an appointment for a conference at your earliest convenience?"

"Jessica doesn't seem quite ready for first grade. She hasn't learned her letter sounds and often has a difficult time paying attention when we read stories in the circle."

"Ken hasn't turned in his science homework for over a week. Can you give me a call right away?"

It took me awhile to realize that the majority of parents have done the very best they know how. It's not as if they purposely raised a child who can't or won't learn or tried to bring up their offspring to break all the rules in the book. So when they're faced with the prospect of their child's problems in school, their stomachs tighten into knots, they relive their own failures as students, and immediately launch into a cycle of self-blame and recrimination or adopt a defensive position that lays the blame squarely on someone else. For parents, finding solutions to the problems with which educators confront them usually involves facing difficult choices about themselves and their children, often requires large investments of time (and money) on the part of everyone involved, and may mean substantial changes in attitudes and behaviors. Tough choices. Hard work.

Problems Identified by Parents

Sometimes, parents identify school problems on their own. The problem may revolve around a poorly constructed curriculum, books and materials they find unacceptable, poor classroom management on the part of their child's teacher, or lack of achievement expectations in their child's classroom or school. School problems that affect the overall positive attitudes of parents about the school or school system can often have a very detrimental effect on their children's abilities to be successful and well-adjusted in the school setting. These problems are often systemic in nature and frequently take major change to remedy.

Problems Identified by Students

The last category of school problems are those identified by the students themselves. If parents are regularly talking with their children and listening to what they say, there are often clues regarding potential problems in their comments.

"The teacher doesn't like me."

"I don't understand a thing that's going on in that class."

"I got a D on my last math test."

"Nobody likes me."

"My lunch was stolen out of my locker."

"I got put back in a lower reading group today."

"I'm in the dumb class."

"I don't understand my homework."

All children complain about school occasionally. Learning to distinguish between a real problem and the everyday ups and downs of life in a school is a critical skill for administrators—and parents. Not every school day will run smoothly for every child, and part of growing up is learning to deal with our imperfect world. But when the complaints are constant and revolve around a central theme or when they begin to affect appetite, sleep habits, or personality, that's a warning that a serious school problem is in the making (McEwan, 1992). Don't try to pass off complaints as unimportant or the figment of a child's imagination. My experiences as a parent, teacher, and administrator have shown me that children are sensitive human beings with important perceptions about their schooling experiences. If for any reason they aren't happy in school, we need to do all we can to get to the bottom of their anxieties. Any problem faced by a child at school is a real problem that must be addressed. Sometimes, all we need to do is listen and empathize.

SOLVING THE PROBLEMS THAT PLAGUE US

Often, however, it's not enough to listen, empathize, and apologize. Eventually you are expected to solve some of the problems that brought angry parents to your office in the first place. Bullying, ineffective instruction, harassment, academic failure, unresponsive staff members, and unsafe conditions cannot be allowed to exist. Oh, you don't have to solve these problems single-handedly. That is never wise. But as the administrator, you alone have the power to gather information, marshal resources, convene meetings, and facilitate problem solving—to implement the exploratory and action strategies. Without your involvement and expertise, most school problems will just fester and worsen.

Exploratory Strategies

During the exploration phase of an encounter with an upset parent, seek to gather more information, understand the problem more completely, and casually offer some possible options. This phase will likely begin during your initial meeting with parents and if necessary continue to a second meeting devoted completely to problem solving.

Take your time.

There is no rule that says every problem needs an immediate solution. Always take time to think; any decision (or upset parent) will benefit from a twenty-four-hour cooling-off period. Never permit parents to back you into the "I've got to know what you're going to do now" corner. "The wise [educator] knows how to create baffles and buffers to buy time, to absorb heat, to promote collective wisdom, to insure [sic] a maximum sense of legitimacy for final decisions" (Bailey, 1971, p. 225). Here are some ways to slow down the action:

- During the meeting, pause and say nothing, to give yourself time to gather your thoughts. During a long pause, you can sip your coffee or check your notes.
- Regroup by taking a few minutes to summarize the information or progress made thus far.
- Never commit to or even suggest an action that involves other individuals (especially teachers) without first consulting with them.
- Ask for time to gather more information or to consult with a superior. This sends the message that you are serious about solving the problem and want to make sure you're fully informed.
- When a meeting is headed nowhere (e.g., information is being repeated, tempers are beginning to flare, and nothing is being accomplished), perhaps it's time to schedule a follow-up meeting. Consider including some experts to help the situation (e.g., a behavior management specialist to discuss some ways to improve time on-task in the classroom, or the librarian to explain the book selection policy of the district).

Ask questions.

Learn the power of asking the right questions to uncover all aspects of a problem. This process can be compared to the party gag of putting a small gift-wrapped box in increasingly larger and larger boxes, wrapping each one more elaborately than the last. Just when the person who is doing the unwrapping thinks he's about to get his "real" present, he discovers that the final box is empty. Sometimes in talking with parents, something similar will happen. Once all of the layers of confusion and misinformation have been peeled away, the problem may be nonexistent.

Ask all of the usual "who, what, where, and why" questions. You may also find it helpful to use statements such as "I'm not sure I understand. Help me to see why this is so important to you." Offer alternative ways of thinking in the form of questions such as these: "Might it work this way?" or "What if we tried this approach?" When all else fails, ask for the parents' advice: "If you were in my place, what would you do?" or "Do you really think that would be a fair way of handling this problem?" Don't be afraid of asking open-ended questions to which you have no suitable answers. But beware of assuming the role of prosecuting attorney in your questioning mode. Clarification, not conviction, is your ultimate goal. There are a number of positive things that can happen as you question parents with whom you're meeting (Brinkman & Kirschner, 1994, p. 46):

> You will gather higher quality information than what is offered.
>
> You can help the other person become more rational.
>
> You can patiently and supportively demonstrate that you care about what they are saying.
>
> You can slow a situation down long enough to see where it's heading.
>
> You can surface hidden agendas and reveal misinformation without being adversarial.

Sometimes, strange and surprising things can happen if you are able to lay aside your own mental models (or paradigms) and consider alternatives. Mental models are "the images, assumptions, and stories that we carry in our minds of ourselves, other people, institutions, and every aspect of the world. Like a pane of glass framing and subtly distorting our vision, mental models determine what we see" (Senge, Kleiner, Robert, Ross, & Smith, 1994, p. 235). Senge (1990) offers a variety of conversational recipes for turning encounters with people who are challenging or disagreeing with us into a discovery of their mental mode. For example, when faced with an impasse, Senge advises asking questions such as "Are we starting from two very different sets of assumptions here? Where do they come from?" or "It feels like we're getting into an impasse, and I'm afraid we might walk away without any better understanding. Have you got any ideas that will help us clarify our thinking?" (pp. 200–201). The notion that a conference with a distressed parent might actually turn out to be a learning experience for you the administrator may be a somewhat revolutionary idea to consider, but drop your defenses and give it a try. Chris Argyris (1986, 1991), the noted organizational theorist, suggests that even the most skilled professionals must often "unlearn" how to protect themselves from being threatened before they can ever become truly effective managers. What Argyris means is that to be truly effective communicators we must learn to control (i.e., unlearn or relearn) the automatic responses our brains and bodies make to a perceived threat, drop our natural defenses that cause us to respond in kind, and disarm upset parents with a calm acceptance and willingness to listen, learn, and even grow.

Open the option door.

Use verbal aikido techniques, similar to those used in martial arts (Crowe, 1999). Aikido practitioners don't stiffen their bodies in resistance when an opponent comes at them. Rather, they move forward and down, taking the "wind out of the sails" of their opposition and diluting the force and effects of a bodily thrust. Rather than telling parents what they can't have or what you won't be able to do for them because of your policies and procedures, suggest some possible options that *might* work. Of course, you will need to be quick thinking lest you make promises you can't keep, but experience helps and so does asking for time to explore and examine some possible options. Use phrases like the following to open that door (p. 173):

Here are some options . . .

What I *can* tell you is . . .

What you *can* do is . . .

Which would you rather have?

Give me some specifics so that I can see how to help you.

Have you tried . . . ?

Undersell and overperform.

This is a classic principle from the business world (Axelrod & Holtje, 1997, p. 37), but it also has applications in your dealings with upset parents. Promise far less than you think you can deliver. If a parent wants a child moved out of Mrs. Smith's room because her son gets stomach aches during math, don't even suggest the possibility that moving him to another classroom is an option. But there is always the possibility that he can go to another fourth-grade classroom for math. Just don't forget to talk it over first with the teachers involved.

Tell a story.

One of the action strategies that I often used when dealing with parents who were distressed about the placement of their children with specific teachers was to tell a story. Story telling is a technique that can help parents benefit from your own personal experiences without feeling as though you are giving advice or telling them what to do (Shinn, 2004). "Let me tell you a very important lesson I learned when I listened to the complaints of one of my children regarding his sixth-grade teacher," I would say, as we explored some of the available options. "He complained bitterly and persistently about the hostility and anger of his teacher. It was never directed specifically at him, but the climate in the room was not conducive to learning. I went to school and made the same request that you are making today—to move my child to another teacher."

The counselor agreed and moved my son to a new class. "But," I told parents, "then he began to complain that he was separated from his friends and didn't know anyone in his new class. We had just traded one problem for another." I kept the story short and sweet and always asked them the questions that I wish I had been more willing to explore during this incident. What if we had worked on the teacher's behavior through appropriate channels? What if we had given my son some strategies for dealing with angry people that no doubt would have helped him forever? One never knows all of the answers, but a good story can raise issues in more subtle and appropriate ways than direct questions can.

Refuse to triangulate.

Often, perturbed parents want the principal or other administrator to do their homework for them. Let me explain. Suppose Mr. and Mrs. X are upset with Teacher Q. Rather than calling the teacher themselves to discuss the issue, they approach you and demand that the problem be solved for them. Your first question should always be, "Have you talked to the teacher about this?" If the answer is "No, we don't want the teacher to know we're complaining," then it's time to let the parents know that you'll be sharing exactly what they've said with the teacher anyway, and it would be far better for them to do it. If the answer to your question is "yes" and the parents can document several attempts on their part to solve the problem with no success, then it's appropriate for you to step in and facilitate communication between the teacher and parent or determine what is standing in the way of the problem being solved. But beware of being triangulated—caught between two people who should be talking to each other but instead, have decided to put you in charge of their problems.

Lower the boom lightly.

There is an art to giving negative news, something you may well be called on to do in the course of meeting with parents who are upset. How do you tell parents that their child is a bully? How do you share the possibility that a child may have a learning disability? How do you communicate to parents who want to blame everything on you that they own a big share of the problem? Very carefully. With tact and gentleness. But with directness. Don't be so afraid of telling the truth that you never get to the point. Gauge how much information parents can comprehend at one time, particularly if the information is coming as a complete surprise to them. Don't babble and generalize. Speak simply and give concrete examples.

Don't tell parents; show them.

I remember well a conference with a second-grade student's parents. They were very angry that Michael had received a detention from the art teacher. Waving their copy of the form in my face, they demanded that I excuse Michael from serving it. "He didn't do it," they stated. Michael, as angelic as his heavenly namesake, smiled sweetly, fully expecting me to fall in line behind his parents. I invited the threesome into my office. The art teacher was not the type who overreacted. She must have had a good reason for her action. She had written a note at the bottom of the form explaining that Michael had hit the student who sat next to him. They gathered around my table—Michael, his mother, and father, all certain that I would see the "rightness" of their request.

"I'd like to hear about what happened in art class, Michael," I began. "Why don't you tell me about it?"

Michael was suddenly having trouble remembering.

"Who sits next to you at your table?" I asked.

"Amy," he answered.

"Why don't we pretend that I'm Amy," I said. "And you can show me exactly what happened."

Reenacting the "crime" appealed to Michael's sense of the dramatic, and he immediately got into the spirit of things, showing me exactly how Amy's arm had rested on the corner of his drawing.

"Do you think she was doing that on purpose?" I asked.

"Nah," he replied, truthful at least in this instance.

"So what did you do?" I asked.

"Well," he said, "I just touched her like this." He cocked his arm back and slammed his elbow full force into my ribs as his parents watched in dismay.

I caught my breath and said, "I see." And so did his parents. They probably wished for a hole to open up in the floor and swallow them up in their embarrassment. They'd been had by a seven-year-old. I was tempted to lecture them and nail Michael to the wall, but I resisted. I thanked them for following up and being concerned about Michael's progress.

"We appreciate your support. Don't ever hesitate to call us with a question or problem," I said. Sometimes, justice truly is served. This "picture" was worth a thousand words.

Don't fight 'em; join 'em.

When parents identify a problem in your school, enlist their help in solving it. When a group of parents came to see me about problems in the lunch room, I applauded their efforts, said we had already been discussing what could be done to make it a more appetizing experience for our students, and asked their help in creating a task force to study the issue. We all came out winners in that situation.

Focus on problems, not personalities.

Stay focused on issues and keep people and their flaws and faults out of the discussion as much as possible. When parents start tearing down people, redirect their attention to solving the problem.

Action Strategies

For those of you who are action oriented like I am, employing the responsive and exploratory strategies can seem like wasted time, in a sense. We feel like we already know the answers and need to get on with it. There may be many instances when that is the case. Parents are reasonable, the problem is a small one, and everyone is in agreement. However, when parents are angry, troubled, afraid, and totally out of control, taking the time to respond and explore is time well spent. Rushing to judgment and action can exacerbate a bad situation, especially if you end up solving the wrong problem. We are, however, finally at the point of getting down to business. Here are the action strategies you've been waiting for.

Solve problems.

The characteristics of good problem solvers are amazingly similar to the qualities one needs to be a good parent or marriage partner: patience, discipline, creativity, continuous improvement, repetition, honesty, and continuous learning (Lynch & Werner, 1992, p. 160). Problem solving is always a part of quality decision making, but solutions do not come without struggle, frustration, and occasional bouts of chaos and messiness from time to time. Every theorist has developed his or her own model of problem solving, but most include some variation of these seven steps as "must-do's":

1. Gather all the facts and define the problem. Rushing to judgment or stating your opinion about a situation before you have listened to the various sides will often result in solving the wrong problem. Very few educational problems need immediate solutions, and the more information you have at your fingertips, the more likely that a quality solution will present itself. Some possible sources of information include observations, test scores, historical data, and consultations with a variety of specialists. Find someone on your student support team whom you trust, and use that individual as a sounding board for thinking out loud.

2. Identify some possible reasons for or sources of the problem. Beware of responding too quickly with your own expertise. You may know exactly what is needed, but even if you are absolutely correct in your assessment, the other parties involved in the problem (e.g., teachers, parents, students) will need time to reach the same conclusion. I've worked with parents who needed several months to recognize what was best for their child, and if we had not given them that time and space, we would have frustrated our ultimate goal of helping the child.

3. Verify the most likely causes. Sometimes, finding a cause is impossible and a waste of everyone's time. In other situations, determining the cause is a guarantee of a quality solution.

4. Identify several possible solutions. Rare is the problem that has only one solution (even in math), so don't get committed to your solution too early in the discussion. You will shut down the creativity of others and may miss the best one.

On the way to determining a solution to the problem, avoid blaming the child, the parents, or the teacher. Assigning blame is counterproductive and anger evoking. Assume that everyone did the best they knew how up to that point. If behavioral changes (in parents, teachers, students) are called for, someone with administrative know-how and leadership will have to provide help for the needy parties (e.g., staff development, behavior management support, parent training, counseling, etc.). Just *telling* people to change doesn't work.

5. Determine the solution that seems best, and then develop an action plan to implement it. An important part of developing an action plan is to make sure that all of the participants know the why, who, what, where, and when of the plan. I have seen many wonderful plans fail for lack of accountability. Everyone should know why the plan has been designed (e.g., to improve homework completion, to raise reading achievement, or to improve a student's time on task). All of the participants (the *who*) should know the exact actions they're supposed to take (the *what* and *how*). Put the behavioral expectations in writing, and make sure everyone has a copy, including the child. Include a time line in the plan (the *when*), and also include the location in which the activities will occur (the *where*). Anything that is left to chance will not happen.

6. Implement the plan. Make sure you give it enough time to work.

7. Evaluate and fine-tune the plan. Look for concrete evidence of success (e.g., more assignments turned in, fewer unacceptable behaviors, more positive interactions between parent and teacher, etc.).

Be forewarned that as you move through the problem-solving process, there are three possible scenarios that can occur: consensus, compromise, or confrontation/capitulation.

If *consensus* is reached, all the players (parent, teacher, principal, child) agree on the nature of the problem and the solution. There could be some minor differences but not enough to hinder solving the problem. Parents are supportive of school personnel's plans, and they are going to do everything they can at home to help. Sharon's case is a perfect example of consensus and collaboration. Everyone agreed that Sharon had a serious problem. She was in third grade and didn't know how to read. She had transferred in from a private school where her learning problems had fallen through the cracks due to constant turnover in teaching personnel during her first-grade year. We tested Sharon, and it was clear that she had a learning disability. We immediately gave her special services and prescribed activities for her parents to do at home. We also talked with Sharon about what her part would be. Everyone followed through and did their part, and by sixth grade, Sharon was reading above grade level and winning awards in reading. Not every problem has such a successful resolution, but it is an example of what can happen when everyone, including the child, cooperates.

Sometimes, there is disagreement as to the nature of the problem or the type of solution that is needed. In that case, a *compromise* may be reached. Both parents and school personnel agree to disagree on one or more issues but do so in the spirit of cooperation and together are able to work for what is best for the child. Compromise was the result of a problem-solving conference held with Mr. and Mrs. Stafford and their sixth-grade daughter, Joanna. Joanna had a serious personality conflict with a newly assigned teacher hired to replace a teacher on maternity leave, and the situation had gone from bad to worse. The new teacher felt that Joanna was an indulged and spoiled adolescent. Her parents felt the new teacher was incompetent. Joanna was driving a wedge between the school and her parents. The principal was caught in the middle. The Staffords wanted an immediate change in her placement but agreed to a temporary plan designed by the teacher, the principal, and Joanna. There wasn't complete support from home, but the Staffords agreed to wait and see before pressing the transfer issue any further. We managed to make it to the end of the school year without bloodshed.

When there is no agreement and little promise for consensus or even compromise, the result is *confrontation or capitulation* or both. If a parent wants a course of action to be taken that school personnel do not find acceptable, or if school personnel want a course of action to be taken that parents cannot support, an impasse is the result. Effective administrators and teachers always keep looking for ways to solve problems, but if an administrator is unwilling to negotiate or a parent is intractable, capitulation is the only answer. Although this is clearly a last resort, finding another schooling option for a child may be the only solution. Remember, however, that the goal of problem solving is to find a way to help each child be successful in the academic, behavioral, and social arenas.

Tell the truth in love.

I call this particular action strategy, "telling the truth in love" because it is only when principals care for and about parents that they are willing to go the extra mile to help parents to confront behaviors that are damaging to them and their children. "A good [principal] will listen to [parents] without judgment, accept the intensity of [their] feelings, respect [their] pain, and express concern. A really good [principal] will, in addition, help [parents] to see our situation in a new way" (Rosen, 1998, p. 167). Telling the truth in love requires courage and a moral commitment to be forthright and honest. The love of which I speak is not the romantic love associated with "falling in love" or the heartwarming, Kodak moment kind of love we experience when watching our children as they drift off to dreamland after a bedtime story. The truth we tell in love is more akin to "tough love" that is willing to confront difficult situations, even when they make us very uncomfortable, for the good of the child.

Telling the truth in love is a way of helping angry parents deal with underlying causes of their anger over which neither you nor the parent have control: (1) the world is not fair, (2) the world is full of imperfection, and (3) you can't give them what they want. Your goal is to help parents discover this truth, because some problems will only be solved when parents change *their* behavior.

Susan Scott (2002) calls encounters like these "fierce conversations." Lest you erroneously assume that Scott's "fierce conversation" is an acrimonious or hostile encounter, consider a sampling of the synonyms for *fierce*, found in *Roget's Thesaurus* (1977): sincere, intense, passionate, and resolute (p. 490). Instead of thinking "fierce lion," think "fierce loyalty." Scott (2002) defines a fierce conversation thus: "one in which we come out from behind ourselves into the conversation and make it real" (p. 7). Often when we have a situation where parents or their children continue to do and say inappropriate things, we set up a meeting with a game plan and the best of intentions and then end up talking too much and saying all the wrong things. We never get to the point, tell the truth, or as a contemporary metaphor puts it—"talk about the elephant sitting in the middle of the table." Sometimes in our desire to avoid offending parents or embarrassing ourselves, we may babble inanely, confusing rather than communicating. But as the old proverb goes: "If you never stepped on anybody's toes, you haven't been for a walk" (Kingsolver, 1995, p. 45). Scott (2002) describes the avoidance of which we are all guilty in this way:

> When there is simply a whole lot of talking going on, conversations can be so empty of meaning they crackle. Memorable conversations include breathing space. Slow down the conversation so that insight can occur in the space between words and you can discover what the conversation really wants and needs to be about. (p. xiv)

Fierce conversations are rarely ever conducted during a first or second meeting with an angry parent. They are generally structured after you have listened, observed, and explored the situation from a variety of angles. Sometimes you discover that you are dealing with an out-of-control and manipulative parent who is quite adept at avoiding the real issues and keeping *you* in a constant state of anxiety. It's time for a fierce conversation.

Scott (2002) suggests a simple but effective six-step process to use when confronting someone about inappropriate behavior: (1) name the issue, (2) select a specific example that illustrates the behavior or situation you want to change, (3) describe your emotions about this issue, (4) clarify what is at stake, (5) identify your contribution to this problem, (6) indicate your wish to resolve the issue, and (7) invite the other person to respond to what you have said (pp. 149–153). Once you have written a simple statement for each of the six steps, verbalizing them should take no more than sixty seconds.

Here's what one principal said in her sixty-second opening statement to a parent who was terrorizing her son's teacher with drop-in visits after school in which she loudly aired her complaints in front of her own child and the members of his class.

Issue:	Mrs. Martin, I want to talk with you about the effect that your verbal outbursts are having not only on your relationship with Miss Jones, Matthew's teacher, but also on Matthew and his ability to concentrate in school.
Example:	Yesterday, outside the classroom, you confronted Miss Jones in a very hostile and accusatory tone of voice about Mathew's science grade. A number of students (including Matthew) as well as parents and teachers heard you.
Emotions:	I'm distressed about this issue and how it reflects on the climate of our school and also how it has impacted Matthew's feelings about his teacher and school. For the past three afternoons, he has been in the nurse's office complaining of a stomach ache.
Clarification:	I don't want your behavior to become grist for the gossip mill. I care about all of the parents in our school community, including you.
Contribution:	I should have talked to you the first time it happened, but I ignored the situation hoping it would go away. I'm sorry. I didn't help you the way I should have.
Desire to Resolve:	I want to resolve this issue today. I'd like to know that when we leave my office today, we won't ever have to discuss this kind of problem again.
Response:	Mrs. Martin, I want to understand what is going on here from your perspective. Talk to me about this problem.

At this point, the principal sits back and stops talking. The rest is up to Mrs. Martin. You will discover that if you can stand the wait, it will be worth it. Be sure to schedule enough time for this meeting so that you won't be antsy while you're waiting for Mrs. Martin to respond. The secret to a successful fierce conversation is to sit expectantly but calmly looking at the person. Don't have a stare-down, but don't fill the silence and let Mrs. Martin off the hook.

If Mrs. Martin says, "I don't have anything to say about this problem right now," then you might say, "Well, if you *did* have something to say, what would it be?" Or say, "Well, just make something up." If Mrs. Martin still refuses to answer, you might say, "I have no idea what's going on here, Mrs. Martin, but I could make a good guess, if you won't talk to me about this problem."

At that point, you might venture a guess about the reasons behind Mrs. Martin's behavior: "Maybe you hated school when you were a kid, and every time you walk through the school door you feel like you're back in elementary school, and you get so mad that you can't hold it in." If that doesn't register with Mrs. Martin, try this guess on for size: "Maybe the teacher said something very rude to you in the beginning of the year and you just can't stand her or the idea of her son being in her classroom, so every time you see her, you do something outrageous to see if maybe she'll get mad at you and you'll have an excuse to ask for your son's transfer out of the class."

At this point, Mrs. Martin will probably be delighted to tell you that she has been under a lot of stress lately since her husband is moving out and that she feels terrible about her behavior and is humiliated by her immaturity and poor judgment. Bingo. Now you and Mrs. Martin can move on to solve this problem.

BEHAVIORS THAT CAN SABOTAGE YOUR GOOD INTENTIONS

There are several responses you might make to parents who are upset that are very likely to backfire on you. Here's the short list of things not to do:

- Don't interrupt. Sit on your hands. Bite your tongue. Even if the person who's talking has made a mistake, don't jump in to correct it.
- Don't take over the conversation in an attempt to keep from hearing about a problem.
- Don't try to change the subject without giving notice that you're about to do so. Because my mind always seems to race off on my own personal tangents during conversations, I fight this no-no vigorously. When I do feel compelled to veer sharply from the agenda, I give the time-out signal from football and warn the person with whom I'm speaking.

But to someone who's upset, changing the subject can be highly inflammatory.

- Never focus on things that can't be changed. Concentrate on the alterable variables over which you, the parents, and the teacher do have control.
- Don't start complaining about your own agenda (e.g., attacking the superintendent or board of education for not giving you enough money to have the programs you want).
- Don't engage in silent combat (e.g., trying to stare the person down without saying a word).
- Don't start rehearsing your answer before you've actually heard and understood what the parent is trying to communicate.
- Don't advise unless you're asked.
- Don't try to persuade parents by implying or stating that you are right and they are wrong.
- Don't try so hard to be neutral that you show no empathy.
- Don't come across as the know-it-all professional.
- Don't talk compulsively and overexplain or you will raise questions in the minds of your listeners.
- Don't let yourself get backed into a corner by a parent who intimidates you. Think before you say "yes" or "no."
- Don't be so intent on smoothing a conflict that you achieve only a superficial resolution.

WHAT TO DO WHEN NOTHING WORKS

In some cases, nothing you do works. You've done everything right, but everything is still wrong, according to the parent. At that point, I have gently suggested that parents try another schooling option. Not in every case, but in some. Here are the guidelines I've used.

When to Stay

Counsel parents to stay where they are when everyone agrees on the problem and is willing to work on a solution. As wise as parents often think they are, they sometimes don't know a good thing. Help them to see that rushing off into an unknown situation before giving all the players a chance to work on a solution to the problem is a mistake. Encourage parents to give a "problem" teacher a chance to make some changes in the classroom. Try to show them the benefits for both child and teacher of working through an issue.

Advise parents to stay where they are when they are fully cognizant that the problem is their child's and that he or she has the ability to do something about it. If the problem is the child's problem and only his or hers, then moving to a new setting will not solve it. Moving will only confirm for children that if they don't want to shape up or conform, all they have to do is complain and Super Mom and Dad will come to the rescue. Sometimes, children do need a fresh start, but give them every opportunity to solve the problem where it started. They will feel better about themselves if they can.

Suggest that parents stay where they are if the school year is almost over. Everyone gets tired after nearly nine months of hard work. Encourage parents to talk about the decision over the summer when life is less pressured. The decision doesn't need to be made overnight.

Explain to parents the benefits of staying where they are if it appears that their child is manipulating the situation to get what he or she wants without a sincere desire to change. Some children are masters of manipulation. They know that if they can convince their parents that the problem belongs to someone else, they won't have to "face the music." This may be a hard sell for the parent whose child can do no wrong, but be direct and honest— and kind—in your assessment of the situation.

If parents are in the middle of a family crisis, caution them about the wisdom of making a change. Making a decision about schooling for a child when a family is in crisis is a big mistake. There might not even be a schooling crisis once the family problem is resolved. Help them to determine if schooling is really the problem or if some other problem is masquerading as a schooling problem. Often, a family counselor can help parents see the situation more clearly.

When to Leave

There are some good reasons for parents to consider transferring out of a school situation. It is hoped that you will be able to solve the problems they face before that has to happen, but sometimes, solving the problem will take longer than parents are willing to wait. Here's what I advise:

Parents should consider transfer when their child is constantly harassed, bullied, or is in danger. The problem of playground bullies exists everywhere, but if teachers and administrators are powerless to deal with them, it's time to transfer. Parents and teachers should teach children strategies for dealing with bullies, but without effective adult support, life will be miserable for a victim. Children who have different values or who are sensitive or gifted can often be singled out for verbal, if not physical, abuse.

Parents might be wise to transfer a child if he or she has become involved with the wrong peer group. Children's friends become more important to them with each passing year of school, and if friends are influencing children to act in unacceptable ways, then parents need to take action. Parents need to be reasonable in their judgments, but if they can document a decline in their child's motivation, attitudes, respect for family rules and moral standards, that is genuine cause for alarm.

If a child is regularly being exposed to drugs, sex, and violence, a transfer is mandatory. If children have to worry about drugs, sex, and violence as part of their daily environment, they will have little time to concentrate on learning. And neither will anyone else.

Parents should definitely consider a transfer when a child is failing, with no hope of rescue. No child should fail in school. There's no reason for it. Perhaps, with a fresh start in a new setting, a child can begin anew.

When parents object to everything that is done, you can politely recommend that they consider another schooling option for their child. There are some parents who major in criticizing everything that happens in a school. They lie in wait, ready to pounce on a library book with a bad word, a teacher who took a misstep, or a policy that is inconsistent. Their children will be much happier if they don't constantly have to worry about how every little thing that happens to them in school is going to affect their parents.

Sometimes, there are unfortunate personality conflicts, and people have said all the wrong things at the wrong times.

Reconciliation and *conflict resolution* are wonderful buzz words, but when an unresolvable conflict between school personnel and parents exists, kids suffer, and parents seriously need to consider leaving. Children know when the people who are important in their lives aren't getting along. They suffer when their parents disagree over things, and they also suffer when their parents and teachers don't agree. Parents must be able to support the schools wholeheartedly.

I recommend to parents that they transfer when the teachers are poor and no one will do anything about it. There are poor teachers everywhere. Some of them are very nice people; they just can't teach. Some of them aren't even very nice. If a child gets one of those and there's nothing the parents can do to get their child into another classroom, they should look for another school. Nothing should stand in the way of their child's learning. There's too much to accomplish to waste a year in an unproductive situation. A child will spend more than a thousand hours in a self-contained elementary classroom during one school year. That's a lot of time to spend with someone who isn't top-notch. Remediating or releasing ineffective teachers takes time, documentation, and due process. In the meantime, some poor class of kids is going to pay the price. I've been there—in both my personal and my professional lives.

SUMMING UP AND LOOKING AHEAD

In Chapters 1 through 3, we have focused on two big ways educators can deal with parents who are angry, troubled, afraid, or out of control in inappropriate ways: (1) we can help to defuse their emotions by employing appropriate responsive and exploratory strategies, and (2) we can facilitate solutions to their problems by employing one ore more action strategies. However, there are also more proactive steps we can take to reduce or even eliminate the out-of-control emotions and sticky situations that create and even foster cultures where anger, misunderstandings, and distrust are everyday occurrences: (1) create a healthy school climate characterized by accountability and communication, and (2) make parents a part of your school team. We'll examine those steps in Chapters 4 and 5.

Creating and
Nurturing a
Healthy School

*There is a subtle spirit that exists in a school, both in the
minds of the teachers and students and in every act, which
may never be exactly described or analyzed, but which even
the most inexperienced observer recognizes when he enters a
school or a classroom.*

—L. J. Chamberlin (as quoted in
Lindelow & Mazzarella, 1983, p. 169)

We usually talk about health in terms of our bodily systems,
but organizations and institutions can also be described
as healthy or unhealthy. Just as in a healthy body, all of the parts
work together to achieve balance, in a healthy organization, there
is also a sense of wholeness and soundness. A healthy organization
provides an environment in which all members of the community
have the capacity to respond to the challenges that bombard the
system every day so that its integrity and wholeness can be maintained. Just as our human body is constantly under attack by a
variety of bacteria and viruses, there are "diseases" that can momen-
tarily or even permanently disrupt the internal balance and health
of a school. Even the healthiest of living things are subject to a

constant barrage of disease-producing microorganisms. But the healthy human or organization is able to respond to disease with anti-oxidants, immune systems, and healing powers. Just as the presence of disease signals our bodies to begin the healing process (e.g., raise the body's temperature to kill germs), the awareness of disruption, distrust, anger, or frustration in an organization should cause its members to immediately mount an offensive against the unwelcome intruders. Knowing just what germs and diseases are most prevalent can help you diagnose and remediate your potentially ailing school. These infectious invaders can come both from without—the virulent viruses that parents carry into your school—and within—the culture and climate that you and your faculty have created together (Steinke, 1996).

THE "VIRULENT VIRUSES"

The viral infections that angry, upset, out-of-control, and totally outrageous parents can bring into your school are much like the viruses that invade the human body. The healthy human body abounds with viruses, and your school will always have some upset parents. For a virus to do any harm in your body, however, it needs to interact with the body's healthy cells. It does this in very clever ways, tricking the host cells into thinking it's something that it's not. The host cell then innocently provides the virus cell with nourishment and a warm place to live, and the virus begins to grow and multiply. A virus has several interesting characteristics that are also found in many out-of-control parents (Steinke, 1996, p. 56):

It cannot say "no" to itself.

It has no boundary and respects no boundary.

It cannot regulate itself; it goes where it doesn't belong.

It has no ability to learn from experience.

It cannot sacrifice for the sake of other cells.

It is an intracellular parasite with no life of its own.

For out-of-control parents to do any serious damage in your school, they need to find the equivalent of host cells, individuals who reinforce and even applaud their behavior (e.g., other parents, teachers, and even you, the principal). In the absence of strong leadership to confront these individuals and hold them accountable for their inappropriate behavior, parental viruses can be fatal. In and of themselves, however, they pose little threat. Here are the potentially serious six:

Clandestine Operations

There's never anything to worry about when everything is being done out in the open, but when people go underground, trouble begins. Secrets, closed meetings, whispering, and gossiping are the hallmarks of this virus. Healthy schools are open environments where honesty and integrity prevail. Individuals who thrive in secrecy are insecure, dependent, and childish. Their hidden agendas, insincerity, hypocrisy, and deception are behaviors that need to be confronted and eliminated. Strong leadership by both administration and staff is needed.

Here's an example: Ruth Rushton, the Parent-Teacher Association (PTA) president, had mounted a smear campaign against a new principal who refused to bow to her power grab. Ruth's tactics were typical of those who thrive on accusations: gossip, a petition drive, and secret meetings. Bringing her campaign out in the open was difficult but not impossible. The principal responded by inviting Rushton, key communicators, and parent leaders to an open forum where she confronted the lies with equanimity and confidence.

The principal refused to accommodate Ruth's unhealthy fusion with the school and her behind-the-scenes machinations; she exposed them in face-to-face meetings, and once again the school regained its healthy status. Remaining silent in the face of clandestine operations gives the unhealthy atmosphere time and room to flourish.

Faultfinding and Blame

Parents who are unwilling to take responsibility for helping to solve problems often turn instead to blaming everyone else. "You haven't taught my child." "If you were doing a better job, my child would have more friends." In their eyes, no matter what the problem, we are responsible for it and supposed to fix it. The "blame virus" needs a host cell to grow, and it will find one in the person of a principal who spends all of his or her time reinforcing the accusations by defending, explaining, justifying, or trying to "fix" it. Healthy leaders are able to recognize the faultfinding virus for what it is and realize that these accusations do not define them or their schools but rather, define the individual doing the accusing. Carriers of the faultfinding virus are easy to identify. Faultfinders will never be happy, even when the problem is solved. Mrs. Michaelson was a big-time carrier of the faultfinding virus. We were to blame for everything, even her health. If her son wasn't having so many problems in school, she wouldn't have high blood pressure. We listened but refused to take ownership of her problems, continually holding both her and her son accountable for their behavior.

Backyard Gossip

Parents who spread every rumor and half-truth blowing in the wind can often contribute to an epidemic of misinformation. Backyard gossip may seem harmless enough in the beginning, but if you have a critical mass of parents in your school who do not seek out the source when there is a problem but instead take it to their backyard bull sessions, you've got a problem. One of the most important ways to deter backyard gossip is by providing everyone with adequate information. As surely as people do not have information, they will make it up. Their alternative to having the truth is to invent something and then react to their invention.

Lies, Half-Truths, and Slander

Parents with this virus often appear to be "righteous," because their manipulative and deceptive behavior is so subtle. They can quickly undermine the trust level in a school and make even the most effective administrators and teachers slightly paranoid and suspicious. I believe this category of parents is the most difficult to handle because their frames of reference are so radically different from ours that we fail to recognize them for what they are—liars. Scott Peck's (1983) book, *People of the Lie*, offers remarkable insights into this virus, and a fierce conversation, discussed in Chapter 2, might just be in order.

Triangulation

The fifth virus is an easy one to overcome once you recognize its symptoms. Triangulation is when you find yourself in the middle of two people who should be talking to each other, but almost without becoming aware of it, you have taken on the role of go-between. Here's how it works. Mrs. Smith comes to you because of a problem her son is having in fourth grade. The teacher doesn't treat her child fairly. She wants you to solve the problem with the teacher (of course, without telling the teacher of her conversation with you). When you ask Mrs. Smith if she's talked to the teacher, of course the answer is no. There is a Swahili proverb that says, "When elephants fight, it's the grass that gets crushed." Guess who's playing the part of the grass in the class play this week! Some parents will try to triangulate because it's the easiest thing to do. If they can shift their anxiety and the responsibility for solving the problem to you, they'll feel terrific and the problem will become yours. Don't let it happen. Always send people to the sources of their anxiety to solve their own problems. Or as a last resort, offer to facilitate a meeting where both parties are present. Now, when the source of a parent's anxiety is the child, a personal problem or mood they have, or a difficult marital situation, no one at school will be able to solve the problem. Set firm boundaries and articulate who really owns the problem. Clearly, it is neither the teacher's nor the principal's.

The Friendly Enemy

The sixth and last virus can put you flat on your back before you realize you've even been exposed. Saboteurs do not wear signs announcing they are out to undermine your leadership or destroy your credibility. They are most often gracious, supportive, and generous with compliments, at least to your face. But their compliments always leave you feeling slightly less than self-confident and wondering just what was intended. As soon as you gain power or popularity, the friendly enemy will begin working to erode your support. These parents don't like the idea of someone being a successful leader in their school. They liked it better when people turned to them for advice. They may well have serious emotional problems that feed their destructive tendencies (Zey, 1990, pp. 134–139).

THE DANGEROUS DOZEN

With sincere apologies to medical professionals everywhere and especially to those among the readers who may have first-hand (and very painful) knowledge of these ailments, I offer the following tongue-in-cheek compendium of "illnesses" that can attack and debilitate the typical school from within.

Paralysis

The symptoms of "paralysis" in a school are seen largely in the inability of anyone to get anything done. Sometimes, the paralysis is the result of administrators who make all the decisions. They hold such tight reins on their organizations that no one can do anything unless the administrators decree it. This behavior forces staff members to put a lid on creativity because good ideas never go anywhere but into the circular file. This kind of paralysis results in a malaise of inaction and uncertainty.

Diarrhea

The principal symptom of "diarrhea" in the school setting is a constant flow of aggressive and abusive words and actions from parents, students, teachers, staff members, and administrators. Oh, there may be a few thoughtful or sweet-tempered souls somewhere in the bunch, but they will soon learn how business is done and get into line to vent along with everyone else. The symptoms of this kind of diarrhea are frequently evidenced by outbursts in public places, swearing, and an occasional show of physical violence.

Chronic Fatigue

When everyone wants somebody else to do something and no one is willing to step up and roll up their sleeves, "chronic fatigue" has set in. This problem could be caused by overwork and burnout, lack of leadership and motivation, or the absence of a meaningful mission and vision. The disease is debilitating, and sympathetic reactions often make it seem more widespread. Boredom and depression often accompany the fatigue, and a feeling of hopelessness may also set in.

Hypertension

Hypertension in the body is often described as a heart attack or stroke waiting to happen. "Hypertension" in a school setting is like a pot that is about ready to boil over. There are lots of fights on the playground, tension in the teachers' lounge, and wrinkled brows in the main office. Everyone feels uneasy, but they aren't sure just why. Griping and complaining are acute. Before long, Mt. Vesuvius will erupt, and all hell will break loose. By then, major damage will have been done, and repair is difficult and costly.

Heart Failure

The symptoms of "heart failure" are lack of empathy, understanding, and caring. Everyone wants to be heard and understood. No one is willing to "walk a mile in another's moccasins," and a frequently heard aphorism is "I'm looking out for Number One."

Lockjaw

"Lockjaw" results in the inability of people to talk to one another about what's really on their minds. Problems are swept under the rug, or they are discussed in informal parking lot meetings but never in public or in an organized fashion. Administrators are the key carriers of this kind of lockjaw, and its spread can be epidemic if a case is a particularly virulent one.

Circulatory Collapse

The decline of appropriate two-way communication channels signals an imminent "circulatory collapse." When information isn't moving accurately and consistently among and between all members of the school community, circulatory collapse has occurred. This disease is exacerbated by gossip and can be fatal if left untreated.

Muscle and Tendon Inflammation

This condition is annoying and pervasive. "Muscle and tendon inflammation" is characterized by intermittent bouts of aggressive and hostile interpersonal communication. What causes or exacerbates this kind of inflammation is frequently a source of bewilderment to those on the receiving end of the aggression. "What set her off?" "I have no idea what's bothering him." "Do you think it was something I said or did?" Just when you're planning for smooth sailing ahead, inflammation will flare up, creating irritability, a decline in self-esteem, and extreme frustration.

Irritable Bowel Syndrome

The principal symptom of this kind of "irritable bowel syndrome" is the presence of chronic complaining and criticism. No matter what anyone does, it's never enough, and it's always wrong. Both apologies and compliments are greeted with disdain, and most irritable-bowel sufferers wear T-shirts with one of two mottoes emblazoned on the front: "The glass is half-empty" or "The sky is falling."

Calluses, Corns, and Bunions

The toughness and misshapenness that characterize real-life calluses, corns, and bunions can also be found in the close-mindedness and rigidity of individuals in the school setting. The inability to soften, relent, give in, or fit in when present in a critical mass of faculty, parents, and students will result in the inability of the school to adopt a new paradigm, restructure, or reform.

Chicken Pox

When seen in the school setting, this common childhood disease takes a slightly different form. The emphasis is on the "chicken" rather than the "pox," its principal symptom being an unreasonable fear of taking a position or providing leadership. This is another one of those diseases that relies on a carrier to expose others to the virus; the administrator is particularly susceptible and can unwittingly infect an entire school population.

Malnutrition

This malady is difficult to diagnose and in its early stages impossible to recognize. It can afflict staff members who don't seek advanced degrees or who sneer at staff development. It can be seen in a watered-down curriculum with low expectations for students. Even the administrator is prone to this kind of malnutrition by thinking that teaching and learning are only for the teachers and kids. The results of educational malnutrition are poor student achievement, low teacher morale and efficacy, and rampant parental dissatisfaction.

A HEALTHY SCHOOL

If your body has a temperature, that's a signal that you're fighting off an infection. There are also ways to take your school's temperature to see if it's fighting off an invasion of dissatisfaction, distrust, and disorganization. If the mercury is rising, treatment could be needed. The sixteen indicators listed in Figure 4.1 describe a healthy school. A scale of descriptors for each indicator as well as directions for scoring the checklist can be found in the Facilitator's Guide at the back of the book.

Are you beginning to get the idea of what a healthy school looks like? When you're trying to nurture one, you have to know what it can look like. Physicians or scientists examining cells under the microscope to determine if disease is present must have a clear picture of healthy cells in mind before they can confirm the presence of a destructive cell. There are several key principles of a healthy school (Steinke, 1996) that sum up the qualities and characteristics we just described in the Healthy School Checklist. These generalizations have applicability to each of the distinct groups of people who live and work in the

Figure 4.1   The Healthy School Checklist

Indicator 1: All students are treated with respect by all staff members, to include principal, teachers, instructional aides, secretary and office staff, custodial staff, bus drivers, and cafeteria workers.

Indicator 2: The principal and staff establish high expectations for student achievement, which are directly communicated to students and parents.

Indicator 3: The principal and staff members serve as advocates for students and communicate with them regarding aspects of their school life.

Indicator 4: The principal encourages open communication among staff members and parents and maintains respect for differences of opinion.

Indicator 5: The principal demonstrates concern and openness in the consideration of teacher, parent, or student problems and participates in the resolution of such problems where appropriate.

Indicator 6: The principal models appropriate human relations skills.

Indicator 7: The principal develops and maintains high morale.

Indicator 8: The principal systematically collects and responds to staff, parent, and student concerns.

Indicator 9: The principal appropriately acknowledges the meaningful achievements of others.

Indicator 10: All staff members, classified and certified, are able to communicate openly with one another and say what they feel.

Indicator 11: The individual abilities, knowledge, and experience of all staff members are fully used.

Indicator 12: Conflict between various individuals (teachers, parents, students) is resolved openly and effectively, and there is a genuine feeling of respect for one another among these groups.

Indicator 13: The entire school community can articulate and is committed to the vision and mission of the school.

Indicator 14: Staff members can express their views openly without fear of ridicule or retaliation and permit others to do the same.

Indicator 15: Staff members can get help from one another and give help without being concerned about hidden agendas.

Indicator 16: The school climate is characterized by openness and respect for individual differences.

school community: parents, students, certified staff, classified staff, and administrators.

Mission and Vision

The healthy school is a purposeful one. There is a clear vision for the future and an immediate mission for tomorrow. There are places to go and things to do, and everyone agrees on what they are.

Separate Yet Connected

The individuals in a healthy school are separate yet connected. In any type of relationship there are two very unhealthy opposite ends of a continuum—the point at which individuals are so intent on having their own way with no compromise that dissolution (or divorce) is the only alternative, or the equally distressing opposite point, fusion, where there is no room for any individual freedom, and everyone must think and speak the "party line." Healthy relationships in schools, like healthy marriage relationships, are characterized by a separateness that allows for differences and dialogues as well as a connectedness that encourages collaboration and consensus. The extremes of fusion and dissolution are equally unhealthy.

Leaders who insist on cloning themselves when hiring faculty or who are only happy when everyone agrees with everything they do are creating a very unhealthy environment for both themselves and staff members.

Metanoia Rather Than Paranoia

Metanoia and paranoia are Greek words referring to states of mind. Metanoia literally means "repentance" or the ability to change one's mind. People with this quality are able to take responsibility for their actions and assume ownership for the impact their inappropriate behaviors may have on others. They do not carry the baggage of anger and grudges forward to each new day. They are able to forgive and forget. In contrast, individuals with paranoia (literally, the state of being out of one's mind) are out of control. They are unable to regulate their behavior and lack a clear definition of self. Whereas paranoia is a bona fide mental disorder, there are many educators and parents who live in a borderline state of suspicion, criticism, and blame. Too many of these folks on your staff or in your parent community can make for an unhealthy school.

Optimism Rather Than Pessimism

In a healthy school, people feel empowered to solve problems, meet challenges, and overcome adversity. This attitude is fostered by shared decision making; individual and group accountability; and the provision of resources, both human and material. The healthy school can heal itself and bounce back from adversity, a natural aspect of organizational growth and change.

Cooperation Rather Than Competition

Cooperation and interdependence are fostered, rather than competition. Teachers keep their doors open, share ideas and materials, and are able to ask for help in solving problems. Most school staffs still have a long way to go in their understanding of teamwork; they don't really believe that they need each other to accomplish a result. Teachers have traditionally been able to shut their doors and do what they do in privacy, and when all is said and done, they are much more comfortable in this role than in working together. Principals who model, affirm, and even reward those individuals who work together for the good of all children are able to create and nurture cooperation. If all of the staff members are working toward a mutually agreed-on vision and mission—such as all staff members being responsible for all of the children and held accountable for the "graduates" of each school (elementary, middle, high school)—teachers will begin to look at teamwork in a completely different light.

Zero Tolerance of Intolerance

A healthy school is caring and compassionate. Meanness, sarcasm, prejudice, and bitterness are identified, discussed, and eliminated. All members of the school community must hear and heed the same message. Teachers need to hear it from administrators; kids need to hear it from teachers, parents, and administrators; and administrators must act as role models for everyone else. Anything less than zero tolerance will allow the weeds of hatred, disrespect, and bitterness to choke out learning and caring.

Maturity and Growth

The healthy school invests time and money in learning for everyone: students, teachers, parents. The leader doesn't protect or rescue people but enables and empowers them. The learning environment I refer to is different from the "book learning" we traditionally associate with school—studying, memorizing, and taking tests. "It starts with self-mastery and self-knowledge, but involves looking outward to develop knowledge of, and alignment with, others on your team" (Roberts, 1994, p. 355).

THE HEALTHY LEADER

The healthy leader is ready to accept a challenge, is flexible, is willing to consider many options, and is able to leap tall buildings in a single bound. Seriously, being a genuine leader calls for strong emotional, physical, mental, and spiritual health. Healthy leadership provides a strong immune system for a school. The healthy leader must have the ability to follow this advice: "To thine own self be true; And it must follow, as the night the day, Thou canst not then be false to any man" (Shakespeare, *Hamlet*, act I, scene iii). The healthy leader has the following characteristics (Steinke, 1996, p. 98):

- Is able to take a position based on values, principles, and beliefs
- Is aware of personal emotions
- Can manage anxiety
- Can manage anger
- Is able to make adjustments in behavior and feelings
- Stays connected to others

- Recognizes and can deal with emotions in others
- Tolerates differences
- Encourages dialogue
- Defines self from within
- Lives with a purpose in mind
- Moves forward
- Stretches and grows
- Is ready for and can cope with the pain that comes with leading

PROMOTING AND MAINTAINING A HEALTHY SCHOOL

The maintenance of a healthy body is a somewhat tedious and often monotonous job requiring time, discipline, and steadiness. Exercising, flossing, taking vitamins and minerals, and eating a healthy diet are practices that many of us engage in sporadically, if at all. Oh, we have bursts of good intentions, but they frequently fall by the wayside under time constraints or sheer boredom. Eventually, however (for some, sooner rather than later), our neglect and carelessness will result in disease, whether it's our gums, our heart, or our bones, and we will find ourselves facing the painful reality that we have unalterably damaged our bodies.

Reread Figure 4.1, the Healthy School Checklist, for specific ideas, and consider the following suggestions as well:

- Hire staff members who are emotionally healthy. Pay attention during the interview process to the emotional health of your candidates. A secretary who can type 150 words per minute and knows every software program in the book but can't empathize with teachers, parents, and students will be worthless. The teacher who graduated Phi Beta Kappa but isn't willing to collaborate and share ideas with a grade level team will be a liability.
- Don't tolerate gossip and innuendo from others and above all, don't indulge in it yourself. When you hear teachers, students, or parents being rude, politely remind them of the standard of conduct in their school—Members of the ABC School Community are always respectful and courteous to

one another. You cannot expect to nurture students of character if adults do not model the character traits to them every day and in every context. When someone attempts to pass on a tasty tidbit of gossip to you, use an answer like this to keep it from spreading: "I'm not interested in rumors or gossip. If I want to know what's happening over at Sunrise School, I'll give the principal a call and ask." As principal, you set the tone; your behavior is the standard to which the members of your school community will rise or fall.

- If you believe that one of your faculty members or parents is mounting a campaign behind your back to spread rumors or stir up trouble, go to that person immediately and have a fierce conversation, as described in Chapter 2 (Scott, 2002).

- Tend to your own emotional health. If you are out of control, build time in your daily calendar for exercise, down time, and lunch. Seek professional help if you find yourself becoming angry, reactive, and unable to respond in appropriate ways.

- Just as the mechanic lowers the dipstick into your engine's crankcase to check the oil level (or did in precomputer days), "dipstick" your school occasionally to see how things are going. Talk to parents, teachers, and students. Send out surveys, or form focus groups. Don't be the last to know that trouble is brewing.

- Share information. A well-informed and knowledgeable staff is more likely to work together. Don't keep people in the dark about important decisions.

- Share the glory. When staff members can work together and share the credit for accomplishments, an organization gains vitality and energy.

- Schedule staff development activities that focus on team building, cooperative learning, conflict resolution, and other topics that force individuals to consider their individual behavior as it affects the school's mission.

- Reward honesty and transparency. When staff members are willing to bring difficult issues out in the open and deal with them, an atmosphere of trust will develop that can help weather times of stress.

STEPS TO TAKE IF YOUR SCHOOL IS SICK

If after reading this chapter you feel that your school may be unhealthy, there are several things you can and should do. Do remember, however, that your school is a system, and you can't isolate or tinker with one aspect of the system without affecting all of the other parts. Here are some suggestions:

Ask the staff, parents, and students what they think is wrong. Use a group process, such as the Force Field Analysis found in the Facilitator's Guide, to identify specific problems that are keeping your school from being a healthy and viable community.

Develop a school mission statement. If you don't know where you're going, chances are good that you won't get there. The development of a mission statement can bring focus and direction to a group.

Take steps to get rid of staff members who are causing problems. If a problem is really serious (incompetent, ineffective teaching), follow the due-process remediation and dismissal plan that is part of your negotiated contract. If the problem is less well-defined but nevertheless troublesome, consider an involuntary transfer. A change of scenery can often shake up a whiner or wake up a late bloomer.

Hire a consultant to conduct an audit. People will often be more honest with an outsider, and an objective professional can diagnose the problem in a relatively short period of time. This exercise will be worth every penny you spend on it.

SUMMING UP AND LOOKING AHEAD

We have accomplished nearly all of the objectives of this book:

- Exploring the reasons why so many parents are upset
- Learning how to defuse the emotions of upset parents
- Examining some ways to explore and solve problems successfully
- Creating a healthy school climate characterized by accountability and communication

Only one task remains—looking at some ways that you can be more proactive with regard to getting and keeping parents on your team. In Chapter 5 you will find fifty-plus ways to do just that.

The Proactive Approach

Fifty-Plus Ways to Build Parental Support

Collaboration is strengthened through weaving the web of personal relationships. Community builders recognize that, as human beings, we need the opportunity to respond personally to each other, and, as importantly, to feel known and "seen" as valued community contributors.

—Brown and Isaacs (1994, p. 516)

This chapter contains a variety of brief suggestions on how to build parental support proactively. Treat the list as you would a buffet or smorgasbord. Browse, sample, and remember what you liked so you can go back later for more. These suggestions are too brief to provide all the answers you will need to implement them. Browse through your Corwin Press catalog for full-length books that cover the topics in more depth. The benefits of building a strong base of parental involvement and support in your school are powerful. I've listed just a few of them here:

- Students are more successful in school when their parents and school personnel work closely and cooperatively.
- Parents will be more supportive and willing to give educators the benefit of the doubt, even in stress-filled and emotional encounters, when there is a history of working together.
- Everyone in the schooling business (parents, teachers, administrators, and students) will benefit from two-way information sharing and collaborative problem solving.

FIFTY-PLUS SUGGESTIONS TO GET YOU STARTED

1. Shared Decision Making

Involve parents in a site-based decision-making group. Many teachers and administrators are wary of inviting parents to sit in on heated discussions about school improvement, but if you provide training and support, you won't be sorry.

Too often, we make decisions that will affect our parent community without ever bothering to ask for parental input. Or worse, we ask for it and don't use it.

2. Survey Your Customers

Do a phone survey in which you contact a random sample of seven to ten families once per grading period. Give the sampling task to someone who won't recognize any of the names on the list, to avoid sampling errors. Once you have the parents on the line, ask them three questions:

a. What are we currently doing at ABC School that is helpful to you and supportive of learning for your child?

b. What are we doing that is interfering with our effectiveness and should be eliminated?

c. Is there anything we should be doing that we're not?

You can phrase the questions any way you choose; just make sure to ask Question b. Send out a thank-you note or post card to the parents who participated, share the good news with your faculty, and fix the problems that are driving parents crazy.

3. Care Enough to Send the Very Best

Design a thank-you note that features your mascot or a line drawing of your school building. Send them to parents who volunteer in the classrooms from time to time. Make sure you develop a checklist of names so that you don't forget anyone! Parents will talk about the notes they received from the principal, and those who volunteer and don't receive a note will wonder why!

4. Management by Walking Around

Keep your antennae waving as you meet with parents. Ask people what they're thinking, how they're feeling, and how their children are doing. You can detect subtle trends, pick up on a snowballing problem, or even receive an unsolicited compliment if you tune in to the informal parent network. Don't avoid parents at the hardware store or the mall. Be available and approachable.

5. Think Ahead

Learn to anticipate problems before they arise. Stay abreast of the education news and do your homework. If you have anticipated a controversial issue and developed policies and procedures in advance of parental concerns, you'll come across as more competent and credible.

6. Key Communicators

Some of the most influential communicators regarding your school are the classified staff. If you're implementing a new program, explain it to bus drivers, crossing guards, cafeteria workers, secretaries, and maintenance staff. They wield considerable influence in the community, and their conversations in grocery stores, barber shops, and the corner diner will help to shape parental and public opinion of your school, for good or ill.

7. Advance Warning

If you're going to make a change at your school, even if it's something as minor (to you) as the direction in which the cars move in the traffic circle, give parents lots of warning. Changing things such as lunch schedules, report cards, course offerings, sports eligibility rules, immunization requirements, or transportation schedules without warning (and sometimes, even with) can put parents in an uproar.

8. A Key Decision-Making Tool

A key tool in making decisions is a well-timed meeting. If you don't have necessary answers, ask for time to do research; then schedule another meeting. Give parents the sense that when decisions are made, they're not made in haste. Even if you don't give them what they want, please consider their input carefully. You may just find yourself changing your mind.

9. Single Parents

Recognize the special needs of single-parent families and even grandparents. Be willing to set aside traditional notions of a "good" family to benefit children who are being raised in more "contemporary" families. Provide child care for social events and parent-teacher conferences so that single parents can more easily attend. Be willing to conduct telephone or e-mail conferences if a face-to-face conference isn't possible.

10. Breaking Up Is Hard to Do

Accommodating the needs of divorced parents often means going out of your way to provide dual report cards and separate parent-teacher conferences, but the payback in good will and support for a child already torn between mom and dad is worth it. Some districts are even willing to ease residency rules while families are in transition. That, of course, is a matter of district policy.

11. Multicultural Outreach

Understanding the cultural contexts of students and families is especially important for building strong school–family bonds. Be sensitive to nonverbal communication cues, such as eye contact, personal space, and personal touch. Enlist the help of community and religious leaders to build bridges with the cultural or ethnic minorities in your attendance area.

12. Home Visits

If your budget and teachers' contract restraints permit, schedule time for home visits, even if only at a few grade levels. If a home visit doesn't seem practical, parents and teachers can meet on more neutral ground, such as the parent's workplace or a restaurant.

13. Good News Travels Fast

Develop a culture in your school that supports, encourages, and even expects a continued staff outreach to parents through home visits, weekly or periodic newsletters, and positive telephone calls.

14. The Welcome Wagon

Ask your teachers to consider writing a welcome letter to be sent to each student before school opens in the fall. The good will generated by this simple albeit time-consuming gesture will amaze you.

15. Read All About It

Publish a schoolwide newsletter that contains articles by and about teachers, students, and parents. You, the principal, should regularly contribute a letter or column, and the focus should always be positive. I personally wrote a weekly question-and-answer column for our community newspaper, which was a perfect vehicle for answering parents' questions as well as those from the public.

16. Let's Party

Plan social gatherings that permit parents, educators, and students to be with each other in informal ways. Possibilities include back-to-school events, such as picnics and potlucks; ethnic celebrations and dances; and welcoming gatherings for new students and parents (e.g., kindergarten, beginning of middle and high school). Holiday breakfasts and events for grandparents or other family members are also marvelous opportunities for strengthening the home-school connection.

17. Put Out the Welcome Mat

Make your school an inviting place to visit. Provide signs that welcome visitors and point them to the office. Create an atmosphere where teachers, students, and other staff members routinely greet school visitors and ask if they can help them. If languages other than English are spoken by parents, make sure that someone is always available to translate. Display student artwork and other class projects to communicate the emphasis on learning that is present in your building.

18. Open House

In addition to social events and informal gatherings, plan regular open-house events to communicate important information about curriculum and to show off student work. Science fairs, art shows, young authors' conferences, and musical concerts give students an opportunity to shine.

19. Curricular Expectations

What do you expect students to know and be able to do when they exit each grade level in your school (kindergarten through twelfth grade)? How well have you communicated that information to parents? Consider publishing a booklet that sets forth the expectations for each grade level or course to let parents know the mission of your school.

20. Read to Me

Open the school library during evening hours for "study hall" or for family story hours. Encourage parents to check out books for their children or for their own personal use.

21. Kudos to Volunteers

Recognize and reward the many parent volunteers who work in your school with their own personalized T-shirts, a yearly luncheon, or recognition in the school newsletter.

22. Teacher Training

Provide training for your staff in how to communicate with parents; how to handle parents who are upset; and how to answer questions parents have about student problems, curriculum, and school policies. Uninformed teachers are public relations disasters waiting to happen. Don't take for granted the abilities of your teachers to use tact, discretion, and common sense in parental encounters. Schedule a staff development session now.

23. The Night Shift

Be sensitive to the needs of dual-career families and unique work demands when you schedule parent-teacher conferences or special events. Alternate yearly musical programs between afternoon and evening performances to give everyone a chance to attend once in awhile. Schedule evening parent-teacher conferences, also.

24. School-Business Partnerships

Team up with local businesses in partnerships. Our school teamed up with an international seed company with headquarters in our attendance area. Certain grade levels took field trips there each year, and students had the opportunity to see their parents at work. Personnel from the company also worked with our teachers to develop research projects in horticulture.

25. Phone Home

Install telephones in teachers' classrooms so they can easily phone parents and parents can reach them. Be sure to include a voice mail option so that incoming calls that arrive during classroom instruction will not disturb the class. Professionals in most businesses have their own phone lines, and this provision for teachers eliminates lost messages and secretarial gridlock.

26. You've Got Mail

Make sure that your school's Web site provides a click-on link to teachers' e-mail addresses. Not every parent will choose to communicate this way, but give them the option.

27. The Twenty-Four-Hour Policy

If possible, return all telephone calls made by parents to school staff members within twenty-four hours or less. Parents grow very anxious when they don't hear from teachers, thinking the worst. Even if you don't have a firm answer to a question or haven't located the information they want, let them know you received their phone call and are working on their requests.

28. The Dog Ate It

Install a homework hot line where students and parents can verify homework assignments. The same system can also accommodate absentee calls and include a calendar of upcoming events. Monitor the homework and project assignments that teachers give. Homework that requires expensive materials and sophisticated power tools could discriminate against parents who don't have the resources, time, or talent to build elaborate Styrofoam models or write the great American novel. The projects do look impressive in the hallways, but what *is* the real purpose of homework?

29. Keyboard Capers

Solicit donations of used computers and make them available to families in your community for a weekly or monthly checkout period. Students who have received training at school will provide the support that's needed at home.

30. The Family That Learns Together

Schedule family math and science nights where parents and students attend together and do hands-on activities. This is a perfect way to introduce parents to a new curriculum or methodology and to build in "quality time" for families. Be sure to provide child care for very small children.

31. School-Community Partnerships

Initiatives such as Drug-Free Schools programs, Neighborhood Helping Hands, Neighborhood Watch, and other crime prevention programs offer perfect opportunities for educators, parents, and community officials (police, fire, municipal governments) to work together.

32. Parents as Learners

Offer workshops for parents (e.g., how to help children become better readers, or how to structure a discipline plan at home). Enlist the help of your school psychologist, behavior management specialist, social worker, and others to conduct the training. Better yet, use a vacant classroom to offer GED, ESL, or computer classes for parents.

33. Career Days

Invite parents to classrooms to talk about their careers. Encourage them to bring along several items they use in their work and to come in their work clothing. Another event that will bring parents (and other relatives) to school is the opportunity to read their favorite stories aloud in a classroom.

34. Habla Español?

Provide important materials to parents in their native languages. Whenever possible, report cards, handbooks, notices of meetings, and all special education documents should be published in the languages spoken by the parents of your students.

35. Speak to Me

Provide translators at important meetings that involve individual students as well as for schoolwide meetings, such as PTA or Home-School Council.

36. The Cable Connection

Use your local-access cable TV station to communicate with parents. One principal I know has a monthly Fireside Chat program and another regularly reads stories aloud via TV. Broadcasting musical concerts and school plays enables parents to enjoy these events if their schedules have kept them from attending.

37. Put Your Money Where Your Mouth Is

If your budget permits, hire a parent liaison or home-school coordinator. This individual can make home visits, conduct parent education classes, and create good will in the community.

38. Computer Literacy

Hold a computer course for parent-student teams in your school's computer lab. Hire one of your staff members to teach the course.

39. Berlitz Comes to School

If other languages are spoken in your school, offer language classes for credit so that more staff members will be able to communicate with parents. Although fluency in a foreign language is a goal that takes some time to achieve, even the smallest gestures of staff members toward communication will be noted and appreciated by parents.

40. A Solid Foundation

Form an educational foundation to enlist the help of parents and community members in raising funds for projects such as minigrants to teachers, scholarships to summer enrichment programs for students, and technology centers.

41. What's the Score?

Hold a yearly meeting to discuss and explain test scores to parents. Invite a representative from a local college or university to your high school to talk about admission requirements and how test scores are used. Or have a representative from the testing company available to talk to parents who want more detailed explanations of statistics.

42. Can We Talk?

Hold regularly scheduled parent conferences at which student progress is discussed and learning goals for the future are formulated (twice yearly is preferable).

43. Preferred Parking

Provide special parking places for parents who visit the building to volunteer or meet with staff. There's nothing more frustrating to parents than having to park miles away from the building or worry about getting a parking ticket.

44. When I Want Your Advice, I'll Ask For It

Form an advisory council that is kept apprised of everything that is happening at school and in turn feeds back suggestions and questions from the school community. Well-trained advisory council members can keep communication flowing and help to quash rumors and untruths.

45. Here's How to Handle a Problem

Publish a "what to do if you have a problem at school" booklet, letting parents know the procedures to follow for solving specific problems and what to expect in the way of help.

46. Plan Ahead

Publish a yearly school calendar that contains information about all of the important events to take place in the year (athletic contests, musical concerts, fund-raising events, beginning and end of marking periods, etc.) Your staff (and parent leaders) will complain the first time you ask them to choose all of their dates a year in advance, but the calendar will help parents plan ahead. Nothing makes parents madder than last-minute schedule changes or event announcements that go astray.

47. Rules of the Road

Publish a school handbook with all the rules, regulations, and information parents and students need to "survive" in your school. Although there are no guarantees that everyone will read what you publish, at least you gave them the opportunity.

48. Talk to Me

Cultivate a communication culture in which teachers are sensitive to the need for immediate communication with parents when student problems arise. Educators have a responsibility to let parents know immediately of inappropriate behavior, missed assignments, class cutting, and so forth.

49. Paid Parents

When you have the opportunity to hire parents in your school and they have the qualifications you need, don't hesitate to do so. You will need to provide training and clear expectations regarding their responsibilities to be discreet, but a loyal parent employee will work twice as hard at a job in his or her child's school than anywhere else.

50. The Volunteer Army

Structure a variety of volunteer opportunities in your school. Don't assume that parents of middle school or high school students won't volunteer. You may not get as many of them as elementary administrators get, but have you asked?

51. Pop the Question

Take every opportunity you have to talk to parents about their children. They have information you need to know, information that can help you do a better job of educating their children. And when parents talk, listen.

52. Reach Out and Touch Someone

I am aware of the pervasive popularity of automated telephone systems with elaborate options. However, when parents call the school (other than to leave a message on a teacher's voice mail), they usually want to speak to someone. Make sure that whoever is answering your school phone is well trained and projects a positive image. This individual should have ready information regarding special events and knowledge about upcoming field trips and should know the whereabouts of key people (administrators, school nurse, psychologist, etc.). Parents who leave messages for you, the principal, would find it helpful to know when you are out of town and will not be getting the message for a period of time. If the necessary evil of voice mail has arrived in your school, instruct staff members to change their reply messages to coordinate with their schedules. I find it most helpful to know whether someone is in or out of the office, if out, when that person is expected to be back, and with whom I can speak if I need a real, live human being immediately.

53. Volunteer Together

Structure school projects, such as clean-up days, fun fairs, or concession booths at athletic events, in which teams of parents and teachers work together. There's nothing like a little hard work to build bonds of friendship.

54. What's in a Name?

Learn as many students' and parents' names as you can. After you've learned all of your students' names, learn something unique about each one. When you meet with a parent, hand out a compliment or two. Nothing will bring smiles to parents' faces faster than good news about their children.

55. A Penny for Your Thoughts

To come almost full circle, I'll end with a variation on Suggestion 2: Send out an open-ended survey to all parents. Use these three questions to find out what your community is really thinking:

a. What are we currently doing that we should continue doing?

b. What are we doing that we should stop doing?

c. What aren't we doing that we should start doing?

SUMMING UP AND LOOKING AHEAD

If you find this list of fifty-plus suggestions somewhat overwhelming, begin by choosing just five ideas that you believe have potential for improving school-community relations. Present them for discussion at your next faculty or PTA meeting. Ask participants to rank them in order of their importance to parent-school relations and identify one to implement. Be sure to listen carefully to their discussion to determine if there are areas other than the ones you have identified that need more immediate attention.

The Conclusion just ahead summarizes the "big ideas" of this book in Ten Goals at a Glance. They will provide helpful reminders of the critical importance of paying close attention to building positive relationships with all parents—but most especially, those who come to your office to share concerns, problems, and issues.

Conclusion

To be aware of a single shortcoming within oneself is more useful than to be aware of a thousand in somebody else.

—The Dalai Lama

I know how many agendas compete for the attention and completion of today's school administrators. I submit, however, that the ten goals described in this conclusion are more important than anything else currently in your daily planner. You may think that your highest priority at the moment is raising achievement in your school, but allow me to suggest that all of your detailed school improvement plans to leave no child behind will fail if you do not bring all of the parents in your school community alongside your efforts—especially the ones who are currently angry, troubled, afraid, or just plain crazy.

In all likelihood, a fair number of these parents have children who aren't doing well in school. You need their unqualified support to bring their children up to grade level. A significant number of parents whose children *are* doing well are nevertheless dismayed by behavioral and academic standards in schools that don't meet their expectations. They are considering home schooling, private school options, or perhaps a charter school. For your school to be their school of choice, you need to find out what's troubling them and if possible fix it. A mass exodus of students from your attendance area could leave you looking for another job. Here then are the ten goals on which to focus in the weeks ahead.

1. Give Parents What They Want

You no doubt cringed when you glanced at this first goal: *Give parents what they want.* You may be thinking that I have taken leave of my senses. However, consider what it is that parents really do want:

- Instructional leadership
- Effective teachers for their children
- Student achievement
- Communication
- Safety and discipline
- Involvement

If you give parents what they want, you will wake up one sunny school morning as the principal of an award-winning school. Parents want "a self-directed instructional leader with a strong intellect and personal depth of knowledge regarding research-based curriculum, instruction, and learning that motivates and facilitates the intellectual growth and development of self, students, teachers, and parents" (McEwan, 2003b, p. 39).

Parents crave teachers who are effective—individuals who have personal traits that signify character, teaching traits that get results, and intellectual traits that demonstrate knowledge, curiosity, and awareness (McEwan, 2002).

Parents want their children to learn and achieve in school. Some parents have expectations that their children will attend highly competitive universities, but most parents just want their children to know and be able to do more this year than they could last year. They want them to learn to read, write, and compute, have some knowledge of history and science, and if they're really fortunate, learn a foreign language. When students spend days and years and get a diploma from high school without a solid academic foundation, parents get understandably upset.

Parents crave communication—not just newsletters that recycle the same tired information, platitudes, and admonitions—but real communication that specifically describes how their children are doing, tells them what's going on at school, and gives them practical and reasonable ways they can help their children at home.

Parents want, deserve, and must have safety and discipline in the schools their children attend. Parents never fully trust principals and teachers who aren't constantly about the business of making sure that the school grounds, hallways, and classrooms are physically and emotionally safe for all children. Educators who are unable to work together to create a warm, inviting, and secure school community are suspect in parents' eyes.

Last, parents want to be involved. They want involvement that goes beyond fund-raisers and booster clubs. They want the kind of involvement that ensures that their voices will be heard, their needs will be considered, and their importance will be valued, even when they make mistakes, get angry, and lose their tempers occasionally.

If you give parents these six intangibles, they will picket when the school board wants to close your school, lobby for a raise for you at school board meetings, and occasionally even indulge your youthful fantasies. When I announced I would be leaving the principalship and moving to the central office, my parent organization planned a parade in my honor. During one of those informal moments at a PTA meeting, I must have confided to someone that I had always wanted to ride in a convertible like the homecoming queen I never was. At a surprise celebration for which I was totally unprepared, the PTA president presented me a tiara with flowing streamers and a magic wand to wave to my adoring subjects and then pointed through the gymnasium door at a brand-new convertible donated for the occasion by a local dealership. The entire student body trooped out to the playground as I climbed in my convertible-for-an-hour, and we rode around the block several times to enthusiastic cheers. I must confess that after that moment, it was downhill all the way. Central office paled in comparison.

2. Be Proactive Rather Than Reactive

No doubt you have already read or skimmed the fifty-plus ways to be proactive with parents found in Chapter 5. You probably have thought of several more to add to the list. The more meaningful proactive steps you take to build positive parent relationships, the fewer angry parents you will have in your school office.

3. Build Relationships

Relationship building with parents is done one parent at a time. Here are some ways to do that:

- Determine parents' interests and strengths. Award-winning former principal Todd White took note of a painter's truck parked in front of his school during parent-teacher conferences and immediately went looking for its owner. He introduced himself and engaged the truck's owner in a conversation about what could be done about the dreadful peeling paint on the school's front doors. You already know the rest of the story (McEwan, 2003b, p. 66).
- Give parents advance warning. Everything that happens at school is of interest to parents. Don't make the mistake of thinking you can ask parents for forgiveness instead of telling them up front what you have planned. That trick only works with superintendents. If you're hiring new staff members, painting the hallways, or rerouting the traffic circle, parents want to know.

4. Tend to Teaching

Your most important responsibility as a principal is to help your teachers be effective. As part of every opening-day meeting you have with teachers, remind them of your expectations of them with regard to parents. Here are some of my expectations that I always shared with new staff members and frequently reviewed for veterans:

- No surprises. I want to be kept informed of any difficulties you encounter with parents, either new or old. I need to be aware of possible problems if I am going to give you the support you need.
- I will support you only if you will be ready to apologize for inappropriate behaviors and ill-advised decisions: whacking a student over the head with a rolled up newspaper, even if it was in fun; going on a spontaneous walking field trip without notifying the office or sending home permission notes; or showing an R-rated movie, even if you did

turn off the video and fast-forward through what you felt were the "R" sections.

- I will not tolerate any blaming of parents when kids don't learn or behave. You may feel this way from time to time, but please do not ever speak the following words within the walls of this school: "If only the parents would . . ." After my years in education, I have come to believe that if parents could, they would. They want to, but they don't know how. They would like to, but they don't feel qualified.

- I want your doors to be open to parents at all times, and I expect that two adult-sized chairs will be placed just inside your door expressly for parents to sit in. Parents need not make special appointments to visit your classroom. They just need to stop in the office and make their presence known and then follow the rules that we have jointly established. I want you to inform me of any parents who abuse this privilege, and I will deal with them immediately.

- There is no excuse for failure to communicate. Don't wait until mid-term to let parents know of an academic problem. Don't wait for bad news to call a parent. Call first with good news or a positive introductory phone call.

- There is no excuse for homework assignments that students are not able to complete independently. Do not send home assignments unless you have already conducted an "I do it; we do it; you do it; apply it" teaching sequence.

5. Don't Hit Your Ball Into the Seven Sand Traps

Perhaps you don't play golf or even watch golf tournaments on television. If so, let me explain what a sand trap is. It is a spot on the golf course that is designed to make the game more challenging. Sand traps slow down your game, decrease the likelihood that you will come out a winner, and use up energy that could be devoted to more productive moves. The seven sand traps listed here can lessen your effectiveness during your encounters with angry parents. Avoid them at all costs:

- The trap of talking too much or too fast
- The trap of interrupting or not listening
- The trap of becoming angry at the angry parent
- The trap of refusing to apologize when you know you should
- The trap of using too much jargon and too many big words
- The trap of getting caught in a power struggle
- The trap of changing the rules or applying them to suit the situation, even if it gives the angry parents what they want

6. Deal With Yourself

If you desire to be the kind of principal about whom parents say, "You can always go to him with a problem," or "She is always looking out for the kids," or "He is a straight-shooter," or "You can trust her," then you must learn to manage your own emotions, behaviors, and attitudes. You must determine where your "hot buttons" are and then diligently work to make sure that no one else ever discovers them.

7. Build a Well-Balanced Team

When staff members work as a team, there will be far fewer angry parents. If the secretarial staff, teaching staff, health office personnel, bus drivers, custodians, and cafeteria workers *all* know what the culture of the school demands of them with regard to their treatment of parents and students, your life will be a bed of roses, so to speak. Well, there may be a few thorns here and there, but there will be far fewer than if everyone does and says just what they feel like doing in any given circumstance.

8. Don't Drive Parents Crazy!

After years of writing newspaper columns and being on talk radio shows, I am certain that in some schools, everyone goes out of their way to drive parents crazy. They seem to specialize in doing the following:

- Not returning telephone calls
- Telling parents to trust them and then abusing that trust
- Stonewalling and circling the wagons to protect inappropriate behavior on the part of staff members
- Stereotyping and treating parents prejudicially
- Acting arrogantly
- Using educational jargon to confuse simple issues
- Defending people who are incompetent
- Lying to parents

9. Tell the Truth in Love

We have an obligation as educators to help parents become better and to help children who are not succeeding. Often that means confronting difficult issues and telling parents that unless we all change what we are doing, their children are on a collision course with serious problems down the road. This is never easy, but you never want to hear parents say: "Why didn't you tell me that a long time ago?" and not have an answer like, "Remember when we had that meeting when Matt was in kindergarten and we talked about where his tantrums and resistant behavior might lead?"

10. Address Small Problems Before They Get Bigger

There *are* rare instances when what appears to be a huge problem resolves itself without intervention. But putting your head in the sand like the proverbial ostrich is generally a recipe for disaster. Hoping that the playground bully will miraculously see the error of his ways just won't happen. Smoking in the girls' bathrooms will not disappear on its own but will likely spawn an epidemic of graffiti. Addressing small problems before they become major ones is essential in schools. Frequently, a minor problem, if ignored, can become an article in the newspaper, a lawsuit at the courthouse, a picket line in front of your school, or the loss of your job.

If you're the kind of person that likes checklists for your bulletin board or daily planner, Figure C.1 displays the Ten Goals at a Glance. If pictures help you to remember as they help me, you'll find a graphic for each goal.

Ten Goals at a Glance

Give parents what they want.

Be proactive rather than reactive.

Build relationships.

Tend to teaching.

Don't hit your ball into the sand traps.

Deal with yourself.

Build a well-balanced team.

Don't drive parents crazy.

Tell the truth in love.

Don't ignore problems; they will usually get worse.

Thank you for reading *How to Deal With Parents Who Are Angry, Troubled, Afraid, or Just Plain Crazy.* I hope that you now feel more confident regarding your ability to deal with difficult parents. Building relationships with parents toward the goal of helping all students grow intellectually, socially, and academically is not only in our job description. It's one of the most enriching aspects of being an instructional leader. One of my favorite research studies is titled *Kids Can't Learn from Teachers They Don't Like.* A corollary study might well test this hypothesis: *Kids Can't Learn When Their Parents and the Principal Don't Get Along.*

References

Advising Forum. (2003, April). *The mentor: An advising journal.* Retrieved June 23, 2004, at www.psu.edu/dus/mentor/foru0304.htm

A lesson on winking at abuse. (1996, November 26). *Chicago Tribune,* p. A16.

American Society of Professional Education. (2004). *Over-indulged children: Dealing with at-risk youth and their enabling parents.* Retrieved April 5, 2004, from www.aspeonline.com

Argyris, C. (1986). Skilled incompetence. *Harvard Business Review, 64,* 74–79.

Argyris, C. (1991). Teaching smart people how to learn. *Harvard Business Review, 69,* 99–109.

Autry, J. A. (2001). *The servant leader: How to build a creative team, develop great morale, and improve bottom-line performance.* Roseville, CA: Prima.

Axelrod, A., & Holtje, J. (1997). *201 ways to deal with difficult people.* New York: McGraw-Hill.

Bailey, S. (1971). Preparing administrators for conflict resolution. *Educational Record, 53,* 225.

Berger, J. (1991, November 27). Matter-of-factly, New York City begins school condom program. *New York Times,* pp. A1, A9.

Berkowitz, L. (1970). Experimental investigations of hostility catharsis. *Journal of Consulting and Clinical Psychology, 35,* 1–7.

Bradley, A. (1997, March 26). Educated consumers. *Education Week,* pp. 33–34.

Branson, R. M. (1982). *Coping with difficult people in business and in life.* New York: Ballantine.

Brinkman, R., & Kirschner, R. (1994). *Dealing with people you can't stand.* New York: McGraw-Hill.

Brown, J., & Isaacs, D. (1994). *The fifth discipline fieldbook: Strategies and tools for building a learning organization.* Garden City, NY: Doubleday.

Brown, K. L. (2003). *The African American parent guide to public school success: The common sense approach to helping your child.* Sacramento, CA: Urban Renaissance Project.

Charles, C. L. (1999). *Why is everyone so cranky?* New York: Hyperion.

Covey, S. (1989). *7 habits of highly effective people.* New York: Simon & Schuster.

Crowe, S. (1999). *Since strangling isn't an option: Dealing with difficult people— common problems and uncommon solutions.* New York: Perigree.

De Bono, E. (1999). *Six thinking hats.* Boston: First Back Bay.

Definition of helicopter parent. (2004). *The Word Spy.* Retrieved April 5, 2004, from www.wordspy.com.

Drucker, P. (2004). *BrainyQuote.* Retrieved June 23, 2004, from www.brainyquote.com

Dulles, J. F. (2004). *BrainyQuote.* Retrieved June 23, 2004, from www.brainyquote.com

Education Consumers Clearinghouse. (2004). Retrieved June 23, 2004, from www.education-consumers.com

Galley, M. (2002, April 3). School letters on students' obesity outrage some parents. Retrieved June 23, 2004, from www.edweek.com

Gay student wins discrimination case. (1996, November 21). *Milwaukee Journal-Sentinel,* p. 23.

Gross, M. L. (2000). *The conspiracy of ignorance: The failures of America's public schools.* New York: HarperPerennial.

Hale, J. (2001). *Learning while black: Creating educational excellence for African American children.* Baltimore: Johns Hopkins University Press.

Harrington, D., & Young, L. (1993). *School savvy: Everything you need to know to guide your child through today's schools.* New York: Noonday.

Hassel, B. C., & Hassel, E. A. (2004). *Picky parent guide: Choose your child's school with confidence.* Ross, CA: Armchair Press.

Holland, R. (1996). *Not with my child you don't: A citizens' guide to eradicating OBE and restoring education.* Richmond, VA: Chesapeake Capital Services.

Horn, S. (1996). *Tongue fu! How to deflect, disarm, and defuse any verbal conflict.* New York: St. Martin's Griffin.

Illinois Loop. (2004). Retrieved June 23, 2004, from www.illinoisloop.org

Informed Residents of Reading. (2004). Retrieved June 23, 2004, from www.iror.org

Keogh, J. (1996). *Getting the best education for your child.* Los Angeles: Lowell House.

Kingsolver, B. (1995). *High tide in Tucson.* New York: HarperCollins.

Kipling, R. (1936). If. In H. Felleman (Ed.), *The best loved poems of the American people* (p. 65). Garden City, NY: Doubleday.

Kottler, J. A., & McEwan, E. K. (1999). *Counseling tips for elementary school principals.* Thousand Oaks, CA: Corwin.

Kunjufu, J. (2002). *Black students. Middle class teachers.* Chicago: African American Images.

Lao-Tzu. (1988). *Tao te ching: A New English Version.* Foreword and Notes by Stephen Mitchell. New York: Harper Perennial. (Original version from the 6th century B.C.E)

Lawsuits that target schools and teachers are part of new wave. (1996, November 11). *Arizona Daily Star,* p. B5.

Ledell, M., & Arnsparger, A. (1993). *How to deal with community criticism of school change.* Denver, CO: Education Commission of the States.

Lewis, W. A., & Bucher, A. M. (1992). Anger, catharsis, the reformulated frustration-aggression hypothesis, and health consequences. *Psychotherapy, 29,* 385–392.

Lindelow, J., & Mazzarella, J. A. (1983). School climate. In S. C. Smith, J. A. Mazzarella, & P. K. Piele (Eds.), *School leadership: Handbook for survival* (p. 169). Eugene, OR: Clearinghouse on Educational Management.

Lindsay, D. (1996, February 14). Telling tales out of school. *Education Week,* pp. 27–31.

Lynch, R. F., & Werner, T. J. (1992). *Continuous improvement: Teams and tools.* Atlanta, GA: QualTeam.

Mack, D. (1997). *The assault on parenthood: How our culture undermines the family.* New York: Simon & Schuster.

Matthews, D. (1996). *Is there a public for the public schools?* Dayton, OH: Kettering Foundation Press.

McElroy, W. (2003, November 25). Zero patience for zero tolerance. Retrieved February 5, 2004, from www.foxnews.com/printer_friendly_story/0,3566,103983,00.html

McEwan, E. K. (1992). *Solving school problems: Kindergarten through middle school.* Wheaton, IL: Harold Shaw.

McEwan, E. K. (1997). *Leading your team to excellence: How to make quality decisions.* Thousand Oaks, CA: Corwin.

McEwan, E. K. (2002). *10 traits of highly effective teachers: How to hire, coach, and mentor successful teachers.* Thousand Oaks, CA: Corwin.

McEwan, E. K. (2003a). *7 steps to effective instructional leadership* (2nd ed.). Thousand Oaks, CA: Corwin.

McEwan, E. K. (2003b). *10 traits of highly effective principals: From good to great performance.* Thousand Oaks, CA: Corwin.

MetLife, Inc. (2003). *The MetLife survey of the American teacher: An examination of school leadership.* New York: Author.

Morgan, R. (2003). *Calming upset customers: Staying effective during unpleasant situations.* Menlo Park, CA: Crisp Publications.

National Center for Education Statistics. (2003). *Violence in U. S. public schools: 2000 school survey of crime and safety. Statistical analysis report.* Washington, DC: U. S. Department of Education. Institute of Education Sciences.

Nemko, M., & Nemko, B. (1986). *How to get your child a private school education in a public school.* Washington, DC: Acropolis.

Newstrom, J. W., & Scannell, E. E. (1980). *Games trainers play: Experiential learning exercises.* New York: McGraw-Hill.

No Child Left Behind Act. (2002, January 8). Pub. L. 107-110 115 STAT.1425 H. R. 1.. Retrieved June 23, 2004, from http://www.ed. gov./nclb

Peck, M. S. (1978). *The road less traveled.* New York: Simon & Schuster.

Peck, M. S. (1983). *People of the lie.* New York: Simon & Schuster.

Persell, C. H., & Cookson, P. W., Jr. (1982). The effective principal in action. In National Association of Secondary School Principals (Ed.), *The effective principal* (pp. 22–29). Reston, VA: Editor.

Peterson, P. E. (Ed.). (2003). *Our schools and our future: Are we still at risk?* Stanford, CA: Hoover Institution Press.

Public Agenda. (2003). *Where we are now: 12 things you need to know about public opinion and public schools.* New York: Author.

Riechmann, D. (1996, October 7). Critics give schools PC rating for strict adherence to rules. *Boston Globe,* p. A4.

Roberts, C. (1994). What you can expect from team learning. In P. Senge, A. Kleiner, C. Roberts, R. B. Ross, & B. J. Smith (Eds.), *The fifth discipline fieldbook: Strategies and tools for building a learning organization* (pp. 353–357). Garden City, NY: Doubleday.

Roget's International Thesaurus (4th ed., Rev. by R. L. Chapman). (1977). New York: Harper & Row.

Rosen, M. I. (1998). *Thank you for being such a pain: Spiritual guidance for dealing with difficult people.* New York: Three Rivers Press.

Saphier, J., & King, M. (1985, March). Good seeds grow in strong cultures. *Educational Leadership, 43,* 67–74.

Saunders, D. (2002, March 29). Schools, yes; fat police, no. Retrieved June 23, 2004, from www.townhall.com

Scott, S. (2002). *Fierce conversations: Achieving success at work and in life one conversation at a time.* New York: Viking.

Senge, P. (1990). *The fifth discipline.* Garden City, NY: Doubleday.

Senge, P., Kleiner, A., Roberts, C., Ross, R. B., & Smith, B. J. (Eds.). (1994). *The fifth discipline fieldbook: Strategies and tools for building a learning organization.* Garden City, NY: Doubleday.

Shinn, L. (2004, January 16–18). *You can be a great storyteller. USA Weekend,* p. 14.

Steinke, P. L. (1996). *Healthy congregations: A systems approach.* Washington, DC: Alban Institute.

Stout, M. L. (2001). *The feel-good curriculum: The dumbing down of America's kids in the name of self-esteem.* New York: Perseus.

Tavris, C. (1978). *Anger: The misunderstood emotion.* New York: Simon & Schuster.

Taylor, G., & Wilson, R. (1997). *Helping angry people: A short-term structured model for pastoral counselors.* Vancouver, British Columbia: Regent College.

Walsh, M. (1996, November 17). Confidential agreement in Berkeley sex-abuse case sparks criticism. *Education Week,* p. 9.

Warren, R., & Kurlychek, R. T. (1981). Treatment of maladaptive anger and aggression: Catharsis vs. behavior therapy. *Corrective and Social Psychiatry and Journal of Behavior Technology, 27,* 135–139.

Wegela, K. K. (1996). *How to be a help instead of a nuisance.* Boston: Shambhala.

White, K. A. (1996, November 13). Colorado voters reject parent-rights measure. *Education Week,* p. 1.

Wildlife Hazards for Campers and Hikers. (2004) Retrieved June 23, 2004, from www.geocities.com/~pack215/animal-safety.html

Williams, S. D. (2004). *One dad's defense of Class I schooling.* Retrieved June 23, 2004, from www.GoBigEd.blogspot.com/

Wolff, D. (2002, May 1). Edu-speak. *Education Week.* Retrieved February 4, 2004, from www.edweek.org

World Net Daily. (2004, February 3). 'Going to hell' gets 7-year-old suspended. Retrieved June 23, 2004, from www.worldnetdaily.com

Zey, M. G. (1990). *Winning with people: Building lifelong professional and personal success through the supporting cast principle.* Los Angeles: Jeremy P. Tarcher.

Index

Facilitator's Guide

WHO SHOULD USE THIS GUIDE?

The facilitator's guide for *How to Deal With Parents Who Are Angry, Troubled, Afraid, or Just Plain Crazy* is designed for the following individuals and groups:

- College and university teachers of School-Community Relations courses who wish to help prospective principals prepare for the challenges of interacting positively with parents
- Leaders of study groups who want to facilitate discussion and reflection among principals with the goal of improving parent-school relations
- Individual principals who want to enhance their personal effectiveness in dealing with parents
- Individual principals who are engaged in self-study as part of personal goal-setting or evaluation processes
- Mentors or coaches who wish to advise and encourage the principals in their interactions with parents

While all of the exercises and activities in this guide have been designed with practicing principals in mind, facilitators who are working with aspiring principals or with classroom teachers can adapt the activities to meet their specific needs in one of three ways:

- Adapt the exercises and activities to the parental communication challenges that are unique to particular job roles (e.g., classroom teacher, media specialist, or psychologist).
- Encourage participants to examine and evaluate the ways in which the administrators with whom they currently work interact and deal with parents.
- Suggest that participants *imagine* themselves on the job as administrators and hypothesize what they *might* do in specific instances in preparation for becoming principals.

HOW IS THE GUIDE ORGANIZED?

The guide contains seven instructional modules, each containing the following components: (1) an energizer to introduce the module and engage participants in group interaction, (2) a personal think-aloud that provides focus and accountability for a think-pair-share activity, (3) a group process activity that explores an issue in more depth, (4) a role-playing activity to give participants the opportunity to observe and reflect on different ways to handle angry parents, (5) a set of questions to encourage dialogue among group participants, (6) an out-of-class action goal or reflective writing activity to be recorded in participants' journals, and (7) a reading assignment from the book.

Select or adapt the exercises and activities to fit the needs of your group, the time you have available, and your own personal facilitation style. Some exercises and discussions may take more than one session to complete, depending on the size and experience level of your group.

WHAT MATERIALS ARE NEEDED?

Materials for Facilitators

Copy of *How to Deal With Parents Who Are Angry, Troubled, Afraid, or Just Plain* Crazy

Name tags for participants

Chart paper and markers

Push pins, masking tape, or sticky chart paper

Overhead projector for transparencies

Timer for role-playing

Copies of the forms, figures, or exhibits for participants, which are noted at the beginning of each module

Miscellaneous materials for the various exercises, also noted at the beginning of each module

Materials for Participants

Copies of *How to Deal With Parents Who Are Angry, Troubled, Afraid, or Just Plain Crazy*

Bound journals in which participants will record reflective writing assignments and class notes

STUDY MODULES

Module 1: Introduction

Materials

Sticky-backed nametags, to be completed by participants

Magic markers

Copies of Personal Think-Aloud 1 for participants

Six hats of different colors (optional)

Assignment to be completed before first meeting

Participants should have read the Preface to *How to Deal With Parents Who Are Angry, Troubled, Afraid, or Just Plain Crazy* before the first meeting.

Energizer: Two Truths and a Lie

In Two Truths and a Lie, individuals share two statements about themselves that are true and one that is not. All of the statements

PERSONAL THINK-ALOUD #1: DEALING WITH ANGRY PARENTS

Describe a particularly vivid encounter with an angry parent that continues to haunt you. Explain the reasons why.

What is *your* biggest challenge in dealing with angry parents?

What strategy do you find to be most helpful when dealing with angry parents?

What do you want to know about dealing with angry parents?

must relate to parent-principal relationships and interactions. Other members of the group try to determine which of the statements is not true.

Ask participants to write down three statements about themselves that describe or relate to their interactions with parents, two of them true and the third false. When all participants have completed their statements, ask for volunteers to read their statements and have group members decide which one is false. If the group is very large, divide it into smaller groups for this activity. The object of this "game" is to fool fellow participants with two outrageous truths and a very sensible and commonplace untruth. For example, I might introduce myself by making the following three statements: I once conducted an emotionally charged parent meeting wearing a bumblebee costume; I have never met a parent with whom I couldn't work; and I once had a temper tantrum in the principal's office at my daughter's school. One outrageous truth, as you already know if you read the Preface, is "I once conducted a highly charged parent meeting wearing a bumblebee costume." I also shamefacedly admit that I had a momentary meltdown in the principal's office.

Personal Think-Aloud 1: Dealing With Angry Parents

A personal think-aloud is provided for each module. As individuals complete their think-alouds, pair them with another participant who is also finished so they can immediately share their observations with one another. When using think-alouds, it is helpful, if possible, to have extra tables and chairs placed around the outside of the room to which pairs who finish their work more quickly can move so they will not disturb others who are still working. Paired think-alouds are very effective to ensure that all group members are accountable for thinking about the issues under discussion as well as to ensure that all participants have an opportunity to share their thoughts regarding a specific question. Remind group members of the importance of attending and listening to their partner without interrupting or thinking of what they will say next. Also, explain that every participant is responsible for jotting down some thoughts to share regarding every question.

Process Activity: Six Thinking Hats

This activity is based on Edward DeBono's (1999) book, *Six Thinking Hats*. DeBono proposes six different colored hats to stand for six thinking styles or problem-solving approaches to help readers appreciate and understand the desirability of having people with different styles as part of one's team. In the context of dealing with angry parents, the thinking-hats approach can be used to help participants understand the various ways in which upset parents approach the issues that are distressing them. When I use this activity with groups, I bring along six hats in the six colors suggested by DeBono, but that is optional since gathering the appropriate hats can be time-consuming and expensive if you don't have a collection at hand from which to choose.

The first objective of the activity is for participants to understand the key attributes of the six thinking hats and to determine which hat they "wear" most frequently during their own thinking and problem solving. Then, through role-playing, participants are asked to "put on" hats of other colors to gain an understanding of how individuals with other thinking styles might approach a problem. Buy or borrow a copy of DeBono's book, not only for this exercise but for use in team-building exercises in the future.

Here are thumbnail sketches of the six thinking styles and a brief description of how some angry parents who "wear" those hats might respond and how their principals who wear other hats might also respond in a problem-solving situation:

- Individuals who are white-hat thinkers rely on facts and figures when they make decisions. Angry parents who wear "white hats" will arrive in the principal's office with research studies, computer print-outs, and advice from experts to support their thinking about an issue and to show how the principal (or central office administrators) are clearly misguided. White-hat parents are certain that the weight of the evidence will surely convince anyone who is logical and that the principal is bound to see things their way before the end of the meeting. That is, unless the principal is a red-hat thinker.
- Red-hat thinkers see the world with emotions and feelings. Angry parents and others who wear "red hats" make judgments and decisions based on their intuition and gut

feelings. Their *emotional take* on a problem at school and how it should be solved is paramount. In their view, the principal's job is to make them *feel* better, and they will have strong opinions about how that should happen. The facts and figures of a white-hat principal will not impress red-hat parents. They know how they feel!

- Individuals who wear "black hats" are cautious and careful in their thinking. They weigh all of the pros and cons and don't want to be pushed into making a decision that might be the wrong one. Black-hat parents are almost always slightly worried about what could go wrong. If pushed for a decision on a revised plan to solve the problem, they will turn around and point out all of the problems that exist with the alternative. Principals who wear red hats and always have an intuitive solution up their sleeves will drive black-hat parents right up the office wall.

- Individuals who wear "yellow hats" are positive and optimistic. Yellow hat parents hardly ever get "angry" or "upset." That's because when they have a problem, they cheerfully come up with a solution and are ready to implement it tomorrow. Yellow-hat parents are wonderful people, but they can drive principals crazy because of their boundless energy and desire to get going. One big problem with yellow-hat parents is evaluation and follow-through. Before one project is over, they've moved on to something new.

- The yellow-hat parents will doubtless be joined by the "green hats" who couldn't care less about whether an idea will work as long as they are feeling creative and generating new ideas. White- and black-hat principals will frustrate yellow- and green-hat parents. The green and yellow hats will have six alternatives for solving a problem and be ready to implement while their black-hat principal is still enumerating the reasons that it won't work and gathering more data.

- Blue-hat thinkers are able to wear all of the different hats with ease and move back and forth between different approaches defining the problem, summarizing, and drawing conclusions. The most effective principals wear blue hats. The dream PTA president is a blue-hat thinker—an individual who can work well with many different kinds of people, use their gifts and talents, appreciate their thinking styles, but ultimately get the job done. Angry blue-hat parents are dangerous unless they are on your team. When aroused and upset, they are quite capable of running an effective campaign for the school board, getting elected, and running the district from behind the scenes.

Structure a role-playing exercise in which you give participants a scenario (e.g., a parent of a child with an ineffective teacher makes an appointment to talk with the principal) and ask for volunteers to play the part of an upset parent wearing one color of hat and the part of a principal wearing a different color. Another variation of the exercise is to present a scenario and then assign the color of hat you want everyone to put on. Discuss what might happen, for example, if a black-hat parent comes to a special education staffing. Ask participants what kinds of strategies would be needed at such a meeting. As you experience the role-playing scenarios in the modules that follow, you will find participants referring to the colored hats and describing their styles and parents' styles using the hat metaphor.

Questions for Dialogue

Remind participants that a dialogue is somewhat different from a discussion. The goal of a dialogue is not to reach a resolution, compromise, synthesis, or closure. The goal is to understand the concepts and ideas more completely. In a dialogue, listening is a form of participation; all participants are asked to listen carefully and to refrain from side discussions.

1. Do you agree with the author's choice of a title for this book? Why? Why not? What title would you have preferred?

2. Are there any other categories of difficult parents that you would like to add to this list? Defend your choice.

3. If you believe that it is indeed possible for parents to change their behaviors and attitudes, give a personal example or two to support your belief.

4. In the reading assignment for the next meeting, Chapter 1, the author lists all of the reasons why parents get angry at

educators. What do you think is the number one reason that *you* have so many upset parents on your doorstep? Or conversely, why (in your opinion) do you have so few upset parents on your doorstep?

5. Agree or Disagree: The best way to handle parents who are upset is to *ignore* them until they get their emotions and tempers under control. Defend your answer.

6. The author suggests that the term *effective,* when used to describe principals, means "getting a desired result from a set of behaviors and attitudes." What results are you looking for as a principal and how have your relationships with parents helped or hindered getting the results you desire?

Role-Playing Scenarios

One of the activities in which the participants engage in the modules that follow is role-playing. This exercise will enable participants to use their acting skills (if they so choose) and also to observe how various individuals differ in how they deal with some highly charged and emotional parents.

1. Divide the whole group into five smaller groups of from three to five members.

2. Ask each group to brainstorm some possible angry, troubled, afraid, or just plain crazy scenarios and then to choose one to reenact in a subsequent meeting. Some individuals in each group will gravitate toward playing the "starring" roles in the play—angry parent and capable administrator. Depending on the scenario created by the group, there may also be small supporting roles, such as the student, a spouse, Aunt Millie who comes along to lend moral support, a staff member, or the parent's attorney. Remind participants, however, that the focus should be on the angry parent and how the principal deals with that individual.

3. One member of each small group should serve as the narrator to describe the plot of the scenario, give helpful background

knowledge, introduce the players, and set the stage for the audience.

4. As part of this first meeting, give the groups time to develop their scenarios and assign roles. Remind them that in a role-play, the acting is more improvisational and does not require lengthy rehearsals or props. Ask for volunteers to sign up to role-play for each of the remaining meetings. Each scenario should take no longer than three minutes.

5. Remind participants that after the role-play has been "performed," group members will ask questions, offer suggestions in a positive way, and debrief regarding what they have observed. Further suggestions for the role-playing activity are included in subsequent modules.

Reading Assignment for Next Meeting

Read Chapter 1. Each module covers one chapter that must be read in advance of a scheduled meeting. The only exception is the last meeting, when the assigned reading is the Conclusion.

Action Goal: Reflective Writing Assignment

Ask participants to reflect on and apply DeBono's thinking hats model throughout the coming week as they have meetings with parents and teachers. Ask them to record how their awareness of this model has changed their approach to listening and working with parents or teachers.

Module 2: Chapter 1.
Why So Many Parents Are Angry, Troubled, Afraid, or Just Plain Crazy

Materials

A set of 3 × 5 cards on which to write various types of angry parents for the Process Activity

Copies of Personal Think-Aloud 2 for participants

pta

PERSONAL THINK-ALOUD #2:
WHEN THE TABLES ARE TURNED

List three behaviors or attitudes that you have recently encountered in your dealings with a customer service representative, in person or on the phone, that have "made you mad."

Specifically describe your feelings and physical reactions.

What behaviors and attitudes would have made your experience more satisfying and positive?

What application can you make from this experience to your own dealings with angry parents?

Energizer: Why Do I Trust You?

Ask the participants to think of an individual who is completely trustworthy. This person can be someone either in the participants' professional *or* personal lives. Ask participants to write the name of the individual on a page in their journals and then write three characteristics that make him or her trustworthy. Poll each person for the traits they have written and collate them on a chart. Then ask the participants to come up with specific behaviors and attitudes that would facilitate the development of trust in them by the parents in their school community.

Personal Think-Aloud 2: When the Tables Are Turned

This think-aloud directs participants to reflect on their experiences in settings where they have been wronged as consumers and then mistreated, in their opinion, by customer service representatives. The questions probe the emotional feelings and physical reactions of participants as well as determining how they would like to have been treated. Without belaboring the issues, take a moment after everyone has completed their think-alouds to summarize the applications that could be made to dealing with angry parents from this exercise.

Process Activity: Table Topics

This process activity is a variation on an exercise called "Walking a Mile in Another's Moccasins" (McEwan, 1997, p. 152) that requires two opposing groups, who are not communicating effectively, to listen to one another and then paraphrase the opposing point of view. In this version, participants will step into the "shoes" of a specific category of parent written on the 3 × 5 card that is given to them. A partner will then present the principal's perspective. Use the exchange between the divorced dad and the former principal found at the end of Chapter 1 as an example. First, the divorced dad described what he thought the school should be doing for him that it was not doing. Then, the principal described what she thought divorced parents should be doing that they weren't doing. Ask each pair to come up with a similar back-and-forth exchange to illustrate the conflicting perspectives.

1. Pass out a parent card and a corresponding principal card to every twosome in your group.

2. Give participants some time to step into the "shoes" assigned to them, and then ask each pair to share what their lives are like and how they would like to be treated. For each pair, begin with the parent's viewpoint and then listen to the principal's. To make this exercise more realistic, suggest that participants assume a parental role that they may have had in their real lives, if they feel comfortable sharing from that perspective. For example, if a participant has a child who has been in the classroom of an ineffective teacher, ask him or her to play that role.

3. Here are some suggested role pairs, but participants can create others relevant to their schools: Divorced Dad or Mom and Principal; Parents of a Behavior Disordered Student and Principal; Parent Whose Child Has an Ineffective Teacher and Principal; Parent Whose Child Is Being Bullied on the Playground and Principal; Parent of Color Who Feels Discriminated Against and Principal; and Parent who Doesn't Speak English and Principal.

Role Playing Scenario 1

As facilitator, you can structure the group observation of the role-play in a variety of ways. For example, before the role-play begins, ask participants to focus on a particular strategy, such as "listening" or "attending." Or, allow the role-play to proceed without any special focus and afterwards bring up specific issues you noticed unfolding in the role-play. It's your call. Remember to set the timer for three minutes. There will always be a group or two that has developed a production worthy of Broadway; you may need to limit their time to be fair to the other groups. Afterwards, debrief.

1. First, quiz the "principal" participant: How do you feel your interaction with the angry parent went? If you could replay this scenario, what would you do differently? Was there any strategy that you tried especially hard to use well? What kinds of feelings and physical reactions did you have during your interaction with the angry parent?

2. Then, quiz the individual who played the parent role. Did the "principal's" strategies work? Or did the principal make you feel angrier or demean you?

3. Last, ask the group members for their feedback: How did the "principal's" behavior make you feel physically? Emotionally? What did you think was particularly effective? What could this "principal" do differently next time to be more effective?

Questions for Dialogue

1. A major issue confronting school administrators today concerns school choice and the importance of creating school cultures that parents will choose for their children. What is your personal response to this issue? What kinds of experiences have you had in your community?

2. Do you feel that the author is overplaying the number and types of angry parents out there?

3. What advice would you give to a brand-new administrator regarding angry parents?

4. What are the most common requests that parents make of you and how do you handle them?

Reading Assignment for Next Week

Read Chapter 2.

Action Goal: Reflective Writing Assignment

Use Susan Scott's (2002) six-step process described in Chapter 2 to compose a sixty-second fierce conversation to use with a parent whose inappropriate behavior needs to be confronted. Ask participants to have their "conversations" ready to deliver to a partner during the energizer portion of the next session.

Module 3: Chapter 2. Defusing and Disarming Out-of-Control Parents

Materials

Copies of Personal Think-Aloud 3 for participants

pta

PERSONAL THINK-ALOUD #3:
REFLECTING ON RESPONDING

With which of the responding
behaviors described in Chapter 2
do you have the most difficulty?

Specifically describe what
problems you have with it.

What steps have you taken to
improve your ability to respond in
this area?

What do you think is standing in
the way of your making changes
in this area of responding?

Energizer: Sixty-Second Fierce Conversation

Pair up and take turns giving your sixty-second fierce conversations to your partner. Debrief in the whole group. Ask if anyone has used his or her sixty-second fierce conversation with an actual targeted parent and what the outcome was.

Personal Think-Aloud 3: Reflecting on Responding

If desired, you can always debrief the think-alouds with the whole group, but the objective of these exercises is to encourage everyone to process a topic personally. Often in discussion groups, even if they are small, one or two participants will hang back, either because they feel their ideas aren't worthwhile or because they didn't do the assignment. The paired think-aloud encourages everyone to process. Walk around as participants are writing down their thoughts to make sure that everyone is on task. The personal think-aloud is a good way to ensure accountability. When I use this activity, there are always a few who are used to wiggling out of group activities and don't write anything down on their papers. I gently confront them with a question like, "What are you thinking about?" and usually get a sheepish grin which tells me they aren't thinking about the assignment. "Do you let the students in your school get away with not thinking about their assignments?" I ask. Another sheepish grin usually follows. "Get going," I admonish gently, and they do. The truly recalcitrant participants (especially if they are administrators) always get calls on their cell phones when they have to think aloud! But I keep prodding, and eventually they discover that processing with a partner can be a very valuable learning experience.

Process Activity: Character Builder Gallery Walk

1. Post one piece of chart paper on the wall for each of the character traits described in Chapter 2: trustworthiness, honesty, authenticity, respectfulness, and forgiveness. Divide the group into triads and conduct a Gallery Walk.

2. Ask each trio to write down one action or attitude by a principal that would demonstrate the quality under consideration. Ask them to be very specific and behavioral in the descriptions.

3. After all participants have written down their contributions, look for obvious trends and patterns.

4. Debrief the findings.

Role-Playing Scenario 2

If there are any problems or unresolved issues from the last role-playing session, bring them up for discussion. Choose a new focus for participants, such as having half of the room watch the angry parent for clues to whether the problem they are presenting is really the problem or whether there are other underlying issues. The other half of the group could watch the principal to see if the language and tone of voice used are accepting and affirming to the parent. It's your call.

Questions for Dialogue: Chapter 2

1. How often do you give parents exactly what they request when they come to you? How do you handle the very touchy issue of assigning students to various teachers?

2. Respond to the following statement made by a principal: "I have always believed the we should love children more than adults in our business. By that, I mean that children's interests should take precedence over staff interests" (J. Ratledge, as quoted in McEwan, 2003b, p. 138). What are the conflicts inherent in this statement? How do you handle them?

3. What kind of mind-set does it take to actually welcome criticism from parents? How does one cultivate that mind-set?

4. What does it mean to lower the boom lightly? What techniques do you use to accomplish this?

5. Can individuals without character be effective principals? Comment and explain.

Assignment for Next Meeting

Read Chapter 3.

Action Goal: Reflective Writing Assignment

Conduct a telephone survey with six parents this week using Suggestion 2 from Chapter 5, Survey Your Customers. Use the feedback you receive from parents to make changes as appropriate. Ask your secretary to randomly choose the six names to avoid the temptation of choosing "easy" parents. Describe the results in your journal.

Module 4: Chapter 3. Solving the Problems That Make Parents Mad

Materials

Copies of Form F.1, Wanted . . . For, for participants

Copies of Personal Think-Aloud 4 for participants

Energizer: Wanted . . . For

The Wanted . . . For activity is designed to encourage participants to think about their own personal values, particularly with regard to their interactions with parents. Although these posters won't be appearing on the walls of the post office in the near future, they could well be used as advertisements to fill your shoes when you retire. Hand out a copy of Form F.1, Wanted . . . For to every participant (McEwan, 1997, pp. 18–19).

By this time, participants should be feeling comfortable with the think-aloud process. Encourage participants to choose a partner with whom they have not previously worked for Think-Aloud 4 (p. 132).

Process Activity: Thinking on Your Feet

Principals are expected to think on their feet as they deal with angry parents. This exercise is called Thinking on Your Feet and has been adapted from *Games Trainers Play* (Newstrom & Scannell, 1980, p. 97).

Prepare 3 × 5 cards on which you have written the following statements that have been adapted from Chapter 1. You can also write statements of your own choosing. Make enough sets of cards to ensure all participants have a card.

- Most problems disappear if you just apply a little benign neglect to the situation.
- Backing teachers *and* making sure that parents and students are treated fairly is like walking a tightrope.

Form F.1   Wanted . . . For

My name is _____

And I am wanted for

    Always being _____

    Having strong needs for _____

    Greatly valuing _____

    Living by the slogan _____

    Treating parents with _____

    Always having _____

    Being able to _____

pta

PERSONAL THINK-ALOUD #4:
MY PROUDEST MOMENT

Describe a particularly difficult problem or parent that you have recently dealt with successfully.

What variables do you think were responsible for the successful resolution of this problem?

What specific advice would you give to someone else who encountered a similar situation in his or her school?

- Parents should be seen and not heard.
- Most parents are too focused on their own children's needs to consider the overall needs of the school community.
- I am willing to reassign a student to another teacher in the middle of the school year if a serious problem arises.
- As a matter of policy I never give parents what they want without putting up a little argument about it.
- There are more parents than ever today with serious personal problems.

Give all participants one of the statement cards, and allow them thirty seconds to collect their thoughts so they can make oral responses to their statements. Then ask participants to get into threesomes and take turns making a thirty-second response to this statement. Make sure that each participant in the group has a different statement.

Debrief after several participants in each group have spoken extemporaneously in their small groups: (1) How did this exercise make you feel? (2) How can you become more confident about thinking on your feet? (3) How *have* you become a more confident extemporaneous speaker?

Questions for Dialogue: Chapter 3

1. As you consider the three types of problem-solving scenarios discussed in Chapter 3, is one more preferable to you than any other? Why?

2. The author suggests some specific steps to follow with parents who have severe problems like addiction or abuse. Are there other steps that you believe should be on the list based on your personal experience? Describe them.

3. Do you feel that the author may have a rather Pollyannaish view of school problems and that your experiences do not reflect what you have read in the book?

4. What do you think of "school choice" and the concept that competition will improve the public schools?

Reading Assignment

Read Chapter 4.

Action Goal: Reflective Writing Assignment

Choose a parent with whom you have a personality clash or one with whom you have failed to make a positive communication connection. Write a paragraph or two describing this individual. Then review the list of responsive strategies in Chapter 2 and use them during your next encounter or exchange with this parent. Record the content of any exchanges or encounters that you have with this parent in your journal.

Module 5: Chapter 4. Promoting a Healthy School

Materials

Copies of Personal Think-Aloud 5 for participants

Transparency or PowerPoint slide of the sample Force Field Analysis (Exhibit F.1)

Copies of Forms F.2, F.3.1, F.3.2, F.3.3, and F.3.4 for participants

Energizer: "I'm Gonna Make You Love Me"

With apologizes to The Temptations who popularized the oldie version of this song title, ask participants to pair up and share their experiences during the past week with difficult parents. Have there been any breakthroughs? Did they find this exercise to be phony and contrived? Did they feel awkward? What worked? What didn't?

Process Activity: Force Field Analysis

To create a school culture as described in the Healthy School Checklist distributed in the handouts, principals must marshal all possible facilitating forces toward a clearly stated goal, while at the same time diminishing, reducing, or eliminating the restraining forces that are standing in the way of creating a healthy school. The force field analysis process is a way to identify the facilitating and restraining forces that impact the achievement of a specific goal (McEwan, 1997, pp. 100–102). For the purpose of this force field analysis, the stated goal is to *create a school culture where parents are valued, respected, and affirmed.*

pta

PERSONAL THINK-ALOUD #5:
THERE'S A LOT OF THAT GOING AROUND

Describe what is going around at your school (i.e., what virulent virus is making the rounds?)

What are you doing (or what could you do) to stamp it out?

How healthy do you think your school is? How do you know?

What "illnesses" do you seem to get rid of that crop up again and again (similar to the common cold)? What can you do about them?

Exhibit F.1   Sample Force Field Analysis

Goal: To become a school in which all parents are valued, respected, and affirmed

Facilitating Forces	*Restraining Forces*
⟶	⟵
Teachers are dedicated, hardworking, and caring.	Some staff members have had bad experiences with abusive parents and are reluctant to go the extra mile for parents.
The principal, although both a newcomer and a novice, is knowledgeable and a good communicator.	Some parents were badly treated by a former administrator, and a lot of anger still exists among some groups of parents.
Staff members understand how important good relations with parents are for students to succeed academically.	Staff members aren't clear regarding what is expected of them by the principal with regard to the amount and type of parent communication.
	There is a lot of difference between teachers and their styles of communication. Some send home weekly letters and others do the minimum.

Form F.2   Force Field Analysis Worksheet

Goal: To create a culture where parents are valued, respected, and affirmed	
Facilitating Forces	*Restraining Forces*
⟶	⟵

Form F.3.1   The Healthy School Checklist: General Directions

---

Write the number of the Descriptor that best describes an Indicator on the line in front of the Indicator on The Healthy School Checklist (Scoring Form).

Indicator 1: All students are treated with respect by all staff members (principal, teachers, secretary, custodial staff, bus drivers, cafeteria workers, etc.).

Scale of Descriptors:

1. There is an overall feeling on the part of most staff members that students are out of control. Some staff members resort to yelling, "getting physical," sarcasm, and meaningless punishments. There are frequent power struggles between students and adult staff members. Some staff members tend to demean students by ignoring problems. Staff members frequently complain about student behavior, a favorite topic of discussion in the teachers' lounge.
2. Although some staff members genuinely respect students and are proactive with regard to troublesome student behavior, they are in the minority. Most teachers feel powerless to change student behavior and treat students with a critical and mean-spirited attitude.
3. Many staff members behave positively and respectfully toward students but are reluctant to defend students or offer positive solutions in the face of their more pessimistic colleagues.
4. Although most staff members behave positively and respectfully toward students, there are several pockets of resistance and negativism on the part of teachers.
5. All staff members feel positively and act respectfully toward all students, even those who are challenging. When difficulties arise, they handle them through appropriate channels (e.g., Teacher Assistance Team, referral, consultation with principal, etc.).

Indicator 2: The principal and staff establish high expectations for student achievement, which are directly communicated to students and parents.

Scale of Descriptors:

---

1. Principal and staff believe that unalterable variables, such as home background, socioeconomic status, and ability level, are the prime determinants of student achievement and that the school cannot overcome these factors.
2. Principal and staff believe that the unalterable variables cited in Indicator 1 significantly affect student achievement and the school has a limited impact on student achievement.
3. Principal and staff believe that although the unalterable variables cited earlier may influence student achievement, teachers are responsible for all students mastering basic skills or prescribed learner outcomes according to individual levels of expectancy. The principal occasionally communicates these expectations in an informal way to teachers, parents, and students via written and spoken communications, specific activities, or a combination of these.
4. Principal and staff believe that although the unalterable variables cited earlier may influence student achievement, teachers are responsible for all students mastering certain basic skills at their grade level and frequently communicate these expectations to parents and students in a formal, organized manner. Expectations for student achievement may be communicated through written statements of objectives in basic skills, written statements of purpose or mission for the school that guides the instructional program, or both.
5. Principal and staff believe that together the home and school can have a profound influence on student achievement. Teachers are held responsible not only for all students mastering certain basic skills at their grade levels but for the stimulation, enrichment, and acceleration of the students who are able to learn more quickly and the provision of extended learning opportunities for students who may need more time for mastery. Expectations for student achievement are developed jointly among parents, students, and teachers and are communicated not only through written statements of learner outcomes in core curriculum areas but in enriched and accelerated programs, achievement awards, and opportunities for creative expression.

Form F.3.1 (Continued)

Indicator 3: Principal and staff members serve as advocates of students and communicate with them regarding aspects of their school life. Behaviors might include lunch with individual students or groups; frequent appearances on the playground, in the lunchroom, and in the hallways; sponsorship of clubs and availability to students who wish to discuss instructional or disciplinary concerns; knowledge of students' names and family relationships(other than just their own classes), addressing the majority of students by name; and willingness to listen to the students' side in faculty-student problems. The preceding list is meant only to be suggestive of the type of behaviors that might be appropriate for consideration in this category.

Scale of Descriptors:

1. Principal and staff do not feel that acting as student advocates is an appropriate role and never interact with students on this basis.
2. Principal and staff feel that acting as student advocates is an appropriate role but feel uncomfortable and rarely do it. They seldom interact with students on this basis.
3. Principal and staff rarely act as student advocates but engage in at least three behaviors that encourage communication.
4. Principal and staff feel that acting as student advocates is an appropriate role and engage in at least six behaviors that encourage communication.
5. Principal and staff feel that acting as student advocates is an appropriate role and engage in at least six behaviors that encourage communication as well as establishing some means of receiving input from students regarding their opinions of school and classroom life.

Indicator 4: Principal encourages open communication among staff members and parents and maintains respect for differences of opinion. The main focus of this indicator is on the behaviors that the principal exhibits that give evidence of maintenance of open communication among staff members and parents and respect for differences of opinion. Behaviors might include an open-door policy in the principal's office, acceptance of unpopular ideas and negative feedback from staff and parents, provision of channels for staff and parents to voice grievances or discuss problems, and provision of channels for staff members and parents to interact with each other. The preceding list is meant only to be suggestive of the type of behaviors that might be appropriate for consideration in this category.

Scale of Descriptors:

1. Principal does not encourage open communication among staff members and parents and considers differences of opinion to be a sign of disharmony among organizational members.
2. Principal supports open communication but is rarely available for informal encounters with staff members or parents. Appointments must be scheduled, meeting agendas are tightly maintained, and the flow of information and opinions is rigidly controlled.
3. Principal supports open communication and is available for informal encounters with staff members and parents. Principal is not responsive, however, to problems, questions, or disagreements and shuts off communication of this nature.
4. Principal supports open communication and is available for informal encounters with staff members and parents. Principal is responsive to problems, questions, or disagreements and encourages staff members and parents to work through differences of opinion in positive ways.
5. Principal supports open communication and is available for informal encounters with staff members and parents. An open-door policy exists with regard to all problems, questions, and disagreements. Principal structures a variety of opportunities for staff members and parents to interact both formally and informally, encouraging interaction among grade levels, departments, and instructional teams.

Indicator 5: Principal demonstrates concern and openness in the consideration of teacher, parent, or student problems and participates in the resolution of such problems where appropriate.

Form F.3.1 (Continued)

Scale of Descriptors:

1. Principal does not wish to be involved in the consideration of teacher, parent, or student problems.
2. Principal is willing to be involved in the consideration of teacher, parent, or student problems but is largely ineffective because of poor communication and human relations skills.
3. Principal is willing to be involved in the consideration of teacher, parent, or student problems and is sometimes effective in bringing problems to resolution. Exhibits average communication and human relations skills.
4. Principal is willing to be involved in the consideration of teacher, parent, or student problems and is usually effective in bringing problems to resolution. Exhibits excellent communication and human relations skills.
5. Principal is willing to be involved in the consideration of teacher, parent, or student problems and is nearly always effective in bringing problems to resolution. Exhibits outstanding communication and human relations skills. Has established procedures jointly with faculty for the resolution of problems.

Indicator 6: Principal models appropriate human relations skills. The main focus of this indicator is the variety of appropriate human relations skills that are exhibited by the principal. Behaviors must include, but not necessarily be limited to, (a) establishing a climate of trust and security for students and staff; (b) respecting the rights of students, parents, and staff; (c) handling individual relationships tactfully and with understanding; and (d) accepting the dignity and worth of individuals without regard to appearance, race, creed, sex, disability, ability, or social status.

Scale of Descriptors:

1. Principal exhibits none of the behaviors described.
2. Principal exhibits only one or two of the behaviors described and often has difficulty with tasks that involve human interaction.
3. Principal exhibits two or three of the behaviors described and is usually successful with tasks that involve human interaction.

---

4. Principal exhibits three or four of the behaviors described and is frequently successful with tasks that involve human interaction.
5. Principal exhibits all of the behaviors described as well as many other behaviors associated with good human relations and is almost always successful with tasks that involve human interaction.

Indicator 7: Principal develops and maintains high morale. The main focus of this indicator is the variety of behaviors exhibited by the principal that contribute to the development and maintenance of high morale. Behaviors might include but are not necessarily limited to involvement of staff in planning, encouragement of planned social events, openness in the dissemination of information, equity in the division of responsibility and allocation of resources, opportunities for achievement, recognition for achievements, involvement of the staff in problem solving, and assistance and support with personal and professional problems.

Scale of Descriptors:

1. Morale is nonexistent in the school building. Principal exhibits none of the behaviors described earlier. There is little unity among staff members, leading to competition, clique formation, destructive criticism, disagreement, and verbal quarreling.
2. Morale is marginal in the school building. Principal exhibits few of the behaviors described. Although fewer visible signs of disunity are evident, faculty members nevertheless do not work well together or have positive feelings about their work.
3. Morale is average. Although there are no visible signs of disunity as seen in Descriptor 1, teachers work largely as individuals, rarely working together cooperatively with enthusiasm and positive feelings.
4. Morale is excellent. Morale-building behaviors by the principal result in teachers working together to share ideas and resources, identify instructional problems, define mutual goals, and coordinate their activities.

Form F.3.1 (Continued)

---

5. Morale is outstanding. Morale-building behaviors by the principal result in teachers working together in a highly effective way while gaining personal satisfaction from their work. Principal has identified specific activities that build morale and systematically engages in these activities.

Indicator 8: Principal systematically collects and responds to staff, parent, and student concerns. The main focus of this indicator is the responsiveness of the principal to the concerns of staff, parents, and students that have been systematically collected. Examples of vehicles used to collect information might include, but are not necessarily limited to, one-on-one conferences, parent or faculty advisory committees, student council, suggestion boxes, or quality circles.

Scale of Descriptors:

1. No information is collected from staff, parents, and students. Principal is unresponsive to concerns of these groups.
2. Although information is sporadically collected from groups, principal is largely ineffective in responding to concerns.
3. Information is systematically collected from at least one of the three groups, and the principal is effective in responding to concerns.
4. Information is systematically collected from at least two of the three groups, and the principal is effective in responding to concerns.
5. Information is systematically collected from parents, faculty, and students; principal is effective in responding to concerns; and information is used in planning and implementing change.

Indicator 9: Principal appropriately acknowledges the earned achievements of others. The main focus of this indicator is the variety of activities engaged in by the principal that demonstrate the ability to recognize the contributions of staff, students, and parents. Activities might include, but are not necessarily limited to, staff recognition programs, student award assemblies, certificates, congratulatory notes, phone calls, recognition luncheons, and newspaper articles.

Scale of Descriptors:

1. Principal engages in no recognition activities.
2. Principal engages in at least one recognition activity for one of the three groups (staff, parents, students).
3. Principal engages in at least one recognition activity for two of the three groups (staff, parents, students).
4. Principal engages in at least one recognition activity for all three groups (staff, parents, students).
5. In addition to a variety of recognition activities, the principal involves all three groups in recognition activities for one another.

Indicator 10: All staff members (classified and certified) are able to communicate openly with one another and say what they feel.

Scale of Descriptors:

1. Discussion is inhibited and stilted. People are hesitant to lay their true feelings on the table and are afraid of criticism, put-downs, and reprisals.
2. A few self-confident or politically connected people speak openly, but most are reluctant.
3. Many staff members speak openly but usually only after a communication trend has been established.
4. Although most communication is open, there are some topics that are taboo, or select individuals inhibit open communication with what they say or do.
5. Discussion is always free-wheeling and frank. There is no hesitation on the part of all staff members to "tell it like it is," even in high-risk discussions and decision making. Staff members feel free to express their feelings as well as their ideas.

Indicator 11: The individual abilities, knowledge, and experience of all staff members are fully used.

Scale of Descriptors:

1. The staff is controlled by one individual who runs the show.
2. A select and chosen few do all the work.

Form F.3.1 (Continued)

> 3. At least half of the staff do something, but the same people are always in charge.
> 4. A majority of the staff participates by doing something, but no effort is made to share or exchange roles.
> 5. All staff members are recognized as having gifts and talents that are fully used in accomplishing building goals, and roles are shared and exchanged.
>
> Indicator 12: Conflict between various individuals (teachers, parents, students) is resolved openly and effectively, and there is a genuine feeling of respect for one another among these groups.
>
> Scale of Descriptors:
>
> 1. People suppress conflict and pretend it does not exist.
> 2. People recognize conflict but do not approach its solution directly and positively.
> 3. People recognize conflict and attempt to resolve it with some success, but they are sometimes clumsy and unskilled in their methodology, resulting in frequent misunderstandings.
> 4. People recognize conflict and can frequently resolve it through appropriate methods, but there are no standardized methodologies for handling conflict.
> 5. People are skilled at recognizing conflict and have a variety of conflict resolution strategies in their repertoire that they use with great success.
>
> Indicator 13: The entire school community can articulate and is committed to the vision and mission of the school.
>
> Scale of Descriptors:
>
> 1. People are openly committed to their own agendas and are unwilling to set aside personal goals for the school mission.
> 2. People pretend to be committed to the mission but frequently work at cross-purposes.
> 3. A core of people (staff and parents) are committed, but a few naysayers and bystanders often work to undermine the mission when it serves their purposes.

4. The majority of people are committed, but no intentional efforts have been made to work through any existing group differences.
5. People have worked through their differences, and they can honestly say they are committed to achieving the mission of the school.

Indicator 14: Staff members can express their views openly without fear of ridicule or retaliation and let others do the same.

Scale of Descriptors:

1. Staff members never express views openly.
2. Some staff members express views openly, but it is usually done with hesitancy and reluctance.
3. Some staff members feel free to express views openly, but many members are reluctant to express their true feelings.
4. Constructive criticism is accepted, but there are no mechanisms for ensuring that it is a regular aspect of teamwork.
5. Constructive criticism is frequent, frank, and two-way; staff members accept and encourage it. Group processes are used that intentionally monitor and encourage the free flow of opinions, ideas, and suggestions for improvement.

Indicator 15: Staff members can get help from one another and give help without being concerned about hidden agendas.

Scale of Descriptors:

1. Staff members are reluctant to admit ignorance or the need for assistance. They are in the "independent" rather than "interdependent" modes.
2. Some staff members will admit to the need for assistance, but many are territorial and competitive.
3. Staff members want to be cooperative but lack the necessary skills.
4. Staff members assist each other, but there is no systematic plan for evaluating the effectiveness of the cooperative atmosphere.

Form F.3.1 (Continued)

---

5. Staff members have no reluctance in asking for help from others or in offering help to fellow staff members. There is transparency and trust among staff members. Processes are used regularly to examine how well the staff is working together and what may be interfering with its cooperation.

Indicator 16: The school climate is one of openness and respect for individual differences.

Scale of Descriptors:

1. Parents and staff members are suspicious and disrespectful of one another.
2. A few parents and staff members are trying to improve the climate but are having a difficult time bringing about change.
3. The majority of parents and teachers work well together, but there are some who attempt to undermine a healthy climate.
4. Parents and staff work well together, but little is done to encourage, develop, and affirm this sense of teamwork.
5. Parents and staff respect and affirm the unique gifts and talents of each individual with appreciation for the variety of learning styles, personalities, and intelligences.

---

1. Display a transparency or PowerPoint slide of the sample force field analysis shown in Form F1 and explain the difference between facilitating and restraining forces.

2. Divide the group into small groups of from three to five individuals and distribute copies of Form F2 for use as a worksheet.

3. Give participants sufficient time to generate a list of both kinds of forces.

4. Then ask each group to select a recorder who will transfer the group's force field analysis to a sheet of chart paper and display it in the room.

Form F.3.2   The Healthy School Checklist: Scoring Form

---

4 Indicator 1: All students are treated with respect by all staff members to include principal, teachers, instructional aides, secretary and office staff, custodial staff, bus drivers, and cafeteria workers.

5 Indicator 2: The principal and staff establish high expectations for student achievement, which are directly communicated to students and parents.

5 Indicator 3: The principal and staff members serve as advocates of students and communicate with them regarding aspects of their school life.

5 Indicator 4: The principal encourages open communication among staff members and parents and maintains respect for differences of opinion.

4 Indicator 5: The principal demonstrates concern and openness in the consideration of teacher, parent, or student problems and participates in the resolution of such problems where appropriate.

5 Indicator 6: The principal models appropriate human relations skills.

5 Indicator 7: The principal develops and maintains high morale.

4 Indicator 8: The principal systematically collects and responds to staff, parent, and student concerns.

5 Indicator 9: The principal appropriately acknowledges the meaningful achievements of others.

4 Indicator 10: All staff members, classified and certified, are able to communicate openly with one another and say what they feel.

5 Indicator 11: The individual abilities, knowledge, and experience of all staff members are fully used.

3 Indicator 12: Conflict between various individuals (teachers, parents, students) is resolved openly and effectively, and there is a genuine feeling of respect for one another among these groups.

3 Indicator 13: The entire school community can articulate and is committed to the vision and mission of the school.

3 Indicator 14: Staff members can express their views openly without fear of ridicule or retaliation and permit others to do the same.

5 Indicator 15: Staff members can get help from one another and give help without being concerned about hidden agendas.

5 Indicator 16: The school climate is characterized by openness and respect for individual differences.

70 Total Score

Form F.3.3   The Healthy School Checklist: Scoring Directions

---

To score an *individual* Healthy School Checklist, total the numbers of the descriptors chosen by the respondent. For example, if Descriptor 3 is chosen for Indicator 1 (All students are treated with respect by all staff members), the score for Indicator 1 is 3; if Descriptor 5 is chosen for Indicator 1, the score for that Indicator is 5, and so forth.

There are two ways to administer and score a *group* of checklists completed by a school faculty or parent group: (1) compute the average rating on the checklist by adding the individual scores of all respondents and then dividing that total by the number of respondents, or (2) compute the average scores on individual indicators on the checklist by adding up the scores of all of the respondents to that indicator and then dividing that total by the number of respondents.

Administering the Entire Checklist to the Faculty or a Group of Parents
If all faculty members or all members of a parent group (e.g., the Parent Advisory Council) complete the entire checklist, their individual scores on the checklist are totaled and then an average is computed.

For example, suppose ten members of the Parent Advisory Council completed the Healthy School Checklist. To compute the average scores of all respondents, add up their total scores and divide by the number of respondents. If ten parents completed the checklist and their ratings totaled 636 (67, 74, 62, 57, 71, 59, 68, 42, 79, 57), divide this total by 10 to compute the average overall rating: 63.6 Then find that score on the Rating Range and determine the rating. In this example, the Parent Advisory Board rated the school as being in Excellent Health. To determine ratings on individual items, see the next set of directions.

Administering Selected Items to the Faculty or a Group of Parents
If input from faculty members or parents is desired on selected items, individual scores are averaged one indicator at a time.

To compute the overall average score for a specific indicator, add up the scores of all of the respondents to that indicator and divide by the total number of respondents. For example, information is desired for Indicators 4 and 7. Ten faculty members were selected at random and asked to choose the most accurate descriptor for Indicator 4 (Principal encourages open communication among staff members and parents and maintains respect for differences of opinion). Their scores were 2, 4, 1, 3, 5, 4, 3, 2, 2, and 1 for a total of 27 and an average of 2.7. This score indicates that a random sample of the faculty feels that the principal needs to open up the flow of communication and be more visible and available to staff members.

The ten members of the Parent Advisory Council were also asked to choose the most accurate descriptor for Indicator 7 (Principal develops and maintains high morale). Their average score was 3.1 indicating that morale is average and that with just a little fine-tuning and encouragement from the principal, the staff could be persuaded to work together and be more supportive of one another.

Form F.3.4 The Healthy School Checklist: Rating Scale

Score	Rating
71-80	Superior Health. Continue to do all of the effective things you are doing, and regularly monitor the vital signs of your school.
61-70	Excellent Health. Even though your school is in great shape, there are a number of actions and behaviors that could notch up its health to Superior.
51-60	Good Health. With some fine-tuning in several areas, your school could be much healthier than it is.
41-50	Poor Health. One more crisis and your school's health will be failing. Change your lifestyle.
40 and under	Intensive care! No visitors until further notice!

5. When all of the force field analyses are displayed, ask the recorder of each group to cross off the restraining forces that are inalterable (e.g., parent demographics or history).

6. Survey the lists together and note the restraining forces that are listed two or more times.

7. Choose one of the common restraining forces and brainstorm ways to minimize or neutralize that force.

8. If any group members have developed successful plans to overcome this force, ask them to share with the group. Point out that when principals use the force field analysis process in their schools, the final step after a specific restraining force has been identified and selected is to develop an action plan to eliminate this restraining force. There is no point in identifying problems if no attempts are made to solve them.

Role-Playing Scenario 3

It's time for another role-playing activity. Address any issues or problems that have arisen during previous role-playing activities. For example, someone may have automatically played the role of the principal using a bombastic, "Don't argue with me, I know best" approach. One response from the group might be to avoid confronting the obvious problems in this kind of approach, leaving unresolved discussion issues. Another response from the group can be a wholesale attack on the role-playing principal, leaving that individual with an uncomfortable feeling. Either way, there is often some unfinished business to take care of. Hopefully in a situation like that, some skilled and highly effective administrator would be able to point out the "principal's" strengths while at the same time highlighting the need for a more empathetic, responsive approach. One of the most effective ways to bring this discussion to the forefront is to ask the individual who played the "parent" role how he or she felt emotionally and physically while the "principal" was telling him or her what to do. This brings the critical issues out into the discussion without having to directly confront the "principal."

Questions for Dialogue: Chapter 4

1. What can happen in a school if the principal regularly triangulates?

2. Describe a "friendly enemy" you have encountered in your school community. How did you handle this individual?

3. What is your response to a "parking lot" meeting? How do they make you feel? What do you do with those feelings?

4. How healthy is your school?

5. What is your response to staff members or parents who are disrespectful to one another, to children, to you?

Reading Assignment for Next Meeting

Read Chapter 5.

Action Goal: Healthy School Checklist

Administer the Healthy School Checklist to your faculty (or to your parent advisory council or PTO board) and be prepared to discuss the results during the Energizer next week. Go over how to administer and score the Healthy School Checklist. Participants may choose to administer the entire sixteen-indicator checklist if time and circumstances permit or select just a few items on which to focus.

Module 6: Chapter 5.
Fifty-Plus Ways to Be Proactive

Materials

Copies of the Personal Think-Aloud 6 for participants

At least four to five pieces each of several kinds of bite-sized candies for the Candyland Process Activity

Energizer: Results of Healthy School Checklist

Divide the group into threesomes and ask them to either share the results of the Healthy School Checklist or talk about issues or problems associated with administering the instrument. Encourage participants to talk about what they plan to do with the information they have gathered. As with the force field analysis, there is no point in asking parents or teachers for input if you do not share the results and then either set personal goals to deal with problems or assemble a small task force to put together a plan.

Think-Aloud 6 (p. 154) is an opportunity for participants to share successful initiatives in their schools. You may want to collate all of the responses and make them available as a resource.

Process Activity: Candyland Brainstorming

Divide the group into several smaller groups by using different varieties of individually wrapped candies. First divide the total number of participants by the number of people you want in each group. For example, thirty-six participants divided by four people in each group will result in nine groups. Purchase four pieces each of nine different types of candy at the supermarket bulk candy counter. Put an assortment of candy pieces in the middle of each table. (Instruct people not to eat the candy until after their

PERSONAL THINK-ALOUD #6:
GIVE YOURSELF A PAT ON THE BACK!

Describe one successful proactive parent initiative you have implemented in your school.

Describe one thing you've changed in your school in response to feedback you've solicited from parents, either recently or in the past.

What's the most significant insight you've gained from this book study thus far?

Facilitator's Guide • 165

groups have been formed.) Ask participants to choose one piece of candy and then find the other participants in the group who have the same variety.

Once the small groups are formed, tell participants that they will be doing a brainstorming activity. Remind them of the basic rules of brainstorming: (1) Quantity of ideas, not quality, is the goal; (2) be freewheeling and creative; (3) make no critical comments or evaluative remarks; and (4) accept all suggestions.

Advise participants that their brainstorming goal is to develop a list of actions and attitudes of principals that would demonstrate to observers that they (or any group of principals) *truly* believe that parents are important members of the school team and their voices should be heard.

Inform the participants that they have three minutes to generate their lists of actions and attitudes. The facilitator will serve as timekeeper, but each group must choose its own recorder to write down the brainstormed items. When the groups have completed their brainstorming, post the lists of behaviors around the room. Give participants time to walk around and look at the lists.

Use the following questions to debrief: (1) What was most difficult about this assignment? (2) What are the implications for making statements like this or having them as part of your mission or vision and not following through with behaviors that give evidence of that belief?

Role-Playing Scenario 4

Summarize what participants have discovered about parent-principal communications during the previous role-plays. If there are strategies that need further discussion (e.g., avoiding distracting body language or holding off suggestions for action until the parent has calmed down), ask participants to look for those in the upcoming role-play. Ask participants what "big ideas" resonate for them thus far about the role-playing experiences. There will always be those who intensely dislike this activity. Find out what their reactions are and explore the reasons for their antipathy, if possible.

Questions for Dialogue: Chapter 5

1. Activities and programs to engage parents sound good. Do they really work? How do you know that they work? What hasn't worked in your school?

2. Do administrators really have time for worrying about parents and how they feel? We can't make them all happy no matter how hard we try. Should we just forget about them and concentrate on kids and their learning?

Reading Assignment

Read the Conclusion.

Action Goal: Reflective Writing Assignment

Ask participants to write a short essay in which they argue for more parent involvement in education *or* less parent involvement in education. Ask them to specify what kind of changes they would recommend if more involvement is needed or to note what they would eliminate if less involvement is called for. Encourage participants to use personal examples and to be prepared to share their essays in the next session.

Module 7: Conclusion

Materials

Copies of Personal Think-Aloud 7 for participants

Copies of Form F.4 for participants

Energizer: Parent Involvement Debriefing

Share the highlights of your essay about parent involvement with a partner.

Think-Aloud 7 provides valuable information for new principals in your group. Collate the responses of the group and make them available as a resource.

Process Activity: Changing Your School's Culture to Make It Parent Friendly

Divide the large group into small groups of from three to five individuals. Saphier and King (1985) suggest twelve norms of school culture that impact school improvement: collegiality; experimentation; high expectations; trust and confidence; tangible support; reaching out to the knowledge base; appreciation and recognition; caring, celebration, and humor; shared decision

pta

Count to ten!

PERSONAL THINK-ALOUD #7:
TAKE IT FROM ME . . .

What advice would you give to brand-new principals to help them be more effective in dealing with angry parents?	
What's one thing you wish you'd known your first year that you know now, after you have some experience?	
What are some ways that you specifically "tend to teaching" in your school?	

Form F.4   Norms of School Culture: Worksheet

Norm: _____

What practices or conditions in your school currently strengthen
this norm?

What practices or conditions in your school weaken this norm?

What is your vision of what this norm would look like at its best?

What specific recommendations do you have to improve this norm?

What would you be willing to do to improve this norm?

making; protection of what's important; traditions; and honest, open communication (p. 67).

1. Assign a different norm of school culture to each of the small groups.

2. Choose the norms that are most likely to affect parent behavior, in the participants' opinions. Use the Norms of School Culture Worksheet (Form F.4) to focus the small-group discussion on the assigned norm.

3. Ask each group to choose a reporter to summarize its findings and conclusions for the whole group.

Role-Playing Scenario 5

After the final role-play is finished and you have debriefed, announce your Academy Awards for the following: Best Actor, Best Actress, Best Supporting Actor, Best Supporting Actress, Best Scenario (Best Writing); Scariest Parent; Most Empathetic, Caring, and Gentle Principal, and so forth. Feel free to add or delete awards from this list, but be sure to pick up some inexpensive trophies or prizes for the winners. And don't forget to give everyone a round of applause for their efforts.

Questions for Dialogue: Conclusion

1. If parents in your community had a choice, would they choose your school? Why? Why not? What might you do in the short term to influence their decisions? In the long term?

2. Would you send your children or grandchildren to your own school? Why? Why not?

3. What characteristics are parents looking for in a school: What do parents want? Or is it impossible to generalize about what parents want?

Concluding Activities and Evaluation

Potluck supper or dinner out at a restaurant

Complete evaluation form

**CORWIN
PRESS**

The Corwin Press logo—a raven striding across an open book—represents the union of courage and learning. Corwin Press is committed to improving education for all learners by publishing books and other professional development resources for those serving the field of K–12 education. By providing practical, hands-on materials, Corwin Press continues to carry out the promise of its motto: **"Helping Educators Do Their Work Better."**